D0014879

ANN TROOLINES DEBRUNCE
387B Carpenteria Rd
Aromas, CA 95004-9709

The
Savior's Touch

Zondervan Treasures

The

Savior's Touch

124 Practical Meditations
with Original Photography by

Charles Stanley

Four best-selling Charles Stanley
devotionals in one volume

ZondervanPublishingHouse
Grand Rapids, Michigan

A Division of HarperCollins*Publishers*

A Touch of His Freedom

Contents

Photographs

*M*y deep appreciation to my son Andy for his able assistance in developing the manuscript and to my friend David Chamblee for his long hours with me in the darkroom.

Introduction

*F*or years my spiritual life was like a roller coaster, up and down, with far fewer ups than downs. I experienced more anxiety than peace, more fear than faith, more emptiness than fullness, and more failure than success.

Was I saved? Yes! Was I free? No! For all practical purposes my new-birth experience had not set me free. I knew the Lord's pardon, but not his freedom. Old habits still harassed me. Twisted emotions still paralyzed me. The power of sin continued to defeat me. Consequently, I knew no joy, only frustration. I longed for the freedom Jesus promised. But for some reason it always eluded my grasp.

My problem was not one of desire. I wished with all my heart to please God. But I was never able to follow through with any consistency. I always felt as if I were fighting a losing battle.

Eventually it dawned on me that I was in bondage; I was a prisoner. The reality of my situation pushed me to the brink of despair. I lived with an overwhelming sense of hopelessness and helplessness.

It was in the early morning hours, after crying out to the Lord throughout the night, that I suddenly realized that I must relinquish to him control of my entire life.

With a deep longing in my heart, I began to search the Scriptures with one objective—to know the joy of real freedom in Christ, freedom to become the person God intended me to be. And I found it. Jesus unlocked the door to my prison cell with six simple words: "The truth will set you free" (John 8:32).

With this promise in my heart I began to apply the principles that follow in this book. In doing so, I experienced a touch of freedom that transformed my life. I pray that God will use this book to expose areas of bondage in your life, and more important, that the truth will set *you* free.

A Touch of His Freedom

*You will know the truth,
and the truth will set you free....
So if the Son sets you free,
you will be free indeed.   John 8:32, 36*

Truth That Sets Us Free

*T*ruth and freedom are constant companions. Where you find one, you will always find the other. Freedom in any area of life comes from discovering the truth about it. And discovering truth in a particular area always results in freedom of some kind.

It is when a child accepts the truth that there is nothing to be afraid of that she is finally free from a fear of the dark. It is only when a little boy accepts the truth that his father can and will catch him that he finds the freedom to leave the security of the diving board and jump into the pool. Likewise, it is only as we accept the truth of all that Christ did for us at Calvary that we will begin to enjoy the freedom he provided.

"The truth will set you free." In six simple words Jesus outlines the process by which any man, woman, boy, or girl can gain freedom in this life. Freedom is not gained through having our way or doing as we please. On the contrary, prisons are full of men and women who simply did as they pleased. These people certainly didn't gain freedom; they forfeited their freedom. And so it is with us every time we carelessly strike out on our own, to do our own thing. What results is not freedom, but bondage.

If I were to ask you whether or not you are free, you may be tempted to answer yes without giving it much thought. But let me ask you this, Are you constantly battling with fear, lust, jealousy, hatred, bitterness, conceit, deceitfulness, a lack of faith, or discouragement? Are there habits in your life over which you seem to have little or no control? Are there certain environments and people you avoid because of an insecurity you cannot overcome? If you answered yes to one or more of these questions, then you are not free. Don't be fooled by the fact that you are not in handcuffs or behind bars.

For the next thirty days we will focus on some specific areas of potential bondage as well as on the truth that provides the way to freedom. As the Holy Spirit brings areas of bondage in your life to the surface, spend some extra time meditating on those truths that correspond to your area of need. And in time, you will be "free indeed"!

Heavenly Father, thank you for providing me with a means by which I can be free. Thank you for paving the way through the death and resurrection of your Son. Now give me insight into your Word that I may uncover the liberating truths I so desperately need to make my freedom complete. And Father, don't let me get discouraged and quit before this journey is complete. Amen.

TOUCHSTONE

Where there is truth, there is freedom.

*You must not eat from the tree
of the knowledge of good and evil,
for when you eat of it,
you will surely die. Genesis 2:17*

Maximum Freedom

*F*or years I believed God was working against my personal freedom. I pictured him as a divine Lawgiver who spent the majority of his time creating new ways to further restrict my liberty. Statements such as the one found in Galatians 5:1 made little sense to me. I would read them over and over and wonder why, if Christ came to set us free, I felt like such a slave.

Then one day while I was reading the first three chapters of Genesis a thought popped into my mind: "Adam and Eve had only one rule." Imagine living in a world where there was only one rule! The implications are astounding. Most significant, however, is the fact that in the perfect environment, where God had everything just the way he wanted it, he issued only one "thou shalt not." To put it another way, God is not a God of rules. Our God is a God of freedom. In the beginning he placed the first man and woman in a beautiful garden and for all practical purposes said, "You are free to enjoy yourselves."

"So," you ask, "why all the moral and ethical taboos now? Whatever happened to the good old days of freedom?" The answer is found in Genesis 3. Our earliest ancestors did the very thing they were told not to do and so opened the door for sin to enter the world. And with sin came death. Thus mankind became a slave to sin and death.

Whereas our world teaches us that freedom is gained through throwing off all restraint, the Scriptures teach that the opposite is true. Human beings forfeited a great deal of their freedom in their attempt to gain absolute freedom. As we begin to put two and two together, it becomes increasingly clear that freedom is gained and maintained by adherence to God's laws. Just as a good father sets loving limitations for his children, so the heavenly Father sets moral and ethical perimeters for us.

Once again, the bottom line is trust. Can we trust that God knows what is best for us? Can we believe that he really has our best interests in mind? Adam and Eve didn't. And they lost the

very freedom they were convinced their sin would ensure them. What about you? Are you willing to accept the fact that God is a God of freedom—that his laws are for your protection, given to ensure, not hamper, your freedom? If so, take a few moments to surrender to God those areas over which you have maintained control. Confess your lack of faith. Now rest in the assurance that God will grant to you the maximum amount of freedom available in this sinful world.

Heavenly Father, thank you for loving me enough to set limits on what I may and may not do. Grant me the wisdom to stay within the confines you have so wisely established. By sending Christ to die you have assured me that you have my best interests in mind. I willingly surrender every area of my life with the assurance that in doing so I am guaranteed freedom. Amen.

TOUCHSTONE

*There is no greater freedom
than that found within the
confines of God's loving
limitations.*

*Anyone who has died
has been freed from sin.*   Romans 6:7

Dead Men Don't Sin

F reedom begins and ends at the cross of Christ. It was at
Calvary that the penalty for our sin was dealt with once
and for all. It was there that Christ was punished on our behalf in
order that we might be free of sin's debt. But something else took
place at the cross that equally effects our freedom. Not only was
the penalty of sin dealt with that day, but the power of sin as
well. Christ's death and resurrection marked the end of sin's
power to control the believer. Just as sin could not control the
Son of God, so it is powerless to control those who have been
placed into Christ through faith.

Unfortunately, many who would nod in agreement with the
above statement are anything but free experientially. They are
still slaves to the same habits and sin that plagued them in their
pre-Christian days. There is no victory over sin. There is little
joy. Consequently, there is little reason to keep struggling. And
so for many believers their motto becomes "Well, nobody's
perfect."

God does not intend for us to continue to live as slaves to
sin. The message of the cross is freedom from sin—both its
penalty and its power. While it is true that we will always be
temptable, it is not true that we must give in to temptation. The
moment you were saved, you were given new life—Christ's life.
You died to your old life; a life dominated by the power and lure
of sin. Your new life is the same life that enabled Christ to walk
this earth for thirty-three years without sinning. It is the very life
that enabled him to walk out of the grave unaffected by death.
On the day you were born again, you became a new person with
a brand new potential in regard to sin and death.

To make this historical and theological truth a reality we
must appropriate it. That is, we must accept it as fact and act on
it. As long as we are convinced to the contrary, we will continue
to live as slaves.

Have you acknowledged your freedom from sin's power?

Have you been claiming it? Or have you been relying on your feelings as indicators of your relationship to sin? Your feelings will tell you that nothing has changed; everything is as it has always been.

But God says you are different. He says you are dead to sin, and dead people are free from the power of sin. Who will you choose to believe today?

> *Heavenly Father, thank you for breaking the power of sin in my life. I want to experience this freedom you have made available. I accept the truth that I am free from sin's power. I am dead to sin and alive to you. I claim ahead of time the victory that is mine in Christ. Remind me of this precious truth as I face the battles this day brings. Amen.*

TOUCHSTONE

We are as free as we dare to believe ourselves to be.

*Do not conform any longer
to the pattern of this world,
but be transformed by the renewing
of your mind. Romans 12:2*

Transformed!

M ost of us have had the frustrating experience of making a sincere commitment only to find that several days later we have abandoned it. I call it the *youth-camp syndrome*. As a teenager I attended church camp just about every summer. As is the case with many camps, we always ended the week with a commitment service. Every year was the same. Everybody cried and promised God the moon—no more lying, cursing, cheating, smoking, drinking, and on and on it went. Unfortunately, most of those promises were broken before we made it back to the church parking lot the next afternoon!

I believe most of the decisions made during those sessions were sincere. The problem was that no one taught us how to follow through. We were clear on the *oughts* and *ought nots*. It was the *how tos* that remained a mystery. Year after year, that one crucial element managed to get left out of those otherwise excellent messages. And consequently, it was left out of our lives as well.

Because of his background, the apostle Paul knew all too well the frustration of knowing what to do without knowing how to do it. No doubt it was his own experience that made him sensitive to his readers' needs in this area. And so in one perfectly penned statement he summarized the key to consistent change: "by the renewing of your mind."

Paul knew that our behavior is directly affected by the way we think. For real change to take place externally, there must first be a change in our thinking. Until we get involved in the process of renewing our minds, any behavioral change is going to be short-lived.

Renewing the mind is a little like refinishing furniture. It is a two-stage process. It involves taking off the old and replacing it with the new. The old is the lies you have learned to tell or were taught by those around you; it is the attitudes and ideas that have become a part of your thinking but do not reflect reality. The

new is the truth. To renew your mind is to involve yourself in the process of allowing God to bring to the surface the lies you have mistakenly accepted and replace them with truth. To the degree that you do this, your behavior will be transformed. The remainder of this book is designed to aid you in this life-changing process.

Heavenly Father, thank you for giving me insight into how I am to go about making the principles of your Word a daily reality in my life. Thank you for not expecting instant change. As I open your Word, guide me to those portions of Scripture that contain the specific truths that I need for renewing my mind today. Thank you for providing such a simple way to ensure my freedom from the world and its destructive influence. Amen.

TOUCHSTONE

Biblical imperatives, apart from biblical thinking, result in short-term obedience and long-term frustration.

Therefore, there is now no condemnation for those who are in Christ Jesus, because through Christ Jesus the law of the Spirit of life set me free from the law of sin and death. Romans 8:1

No Condemnation

*D*o you believe God likes you? "Don't you mean, 'loves me'?" you ask. No, *likes* you. Do you believe God likes you? This is one of my favorite questions. The reason is that it cuts through to the core of how an individual really believes God feels about him or her. So, do you think God likes you? If he were to show up in bodily form, do you think he would seek you out? Would you be someone he would enjoy being around?

Isn't it strange how much more comfortable we are with the concept of *love* than with the concept of *like* when it comes to God's feelings toward us? Why do you think that is true? Often the reason lies in the fact that we have not come to grips with the real extent to which God has forgiven us. Consequently, we live with a subtle sense of condemnation. It's as if there is always a dark cloud separating us from God. We say we are forgiven, but in our hearts we are never fully convinced that God isn't still a little angry with us.

The truth is, every reason God had for being angry with us was dealt with at Calvary. Our forgiveness is so complete that God is not only free to love us, he can like us as well. Think about this: "There is now no condemnation for those who are in Christ Jesus." If you have placed your trust in Christ for the forgiveness of your sins, the Bible says you are positionally in Christ. And once you were placed into Christ, you were separated from the guilt that once brought divine condemnation. You are not condemned. Christ was condemned on your behalf, and now you are free!

"But," you ask, "why do I feel so condemned? Why don't I feel forgiven?" It's probably because you have not made up your mind to take God at his word. Instead, you have measured your worthiness and acceptability by your performance. To be free from feelings of condemnation you must renew your mind to this powerful truth: "There is *now* no condemnation for those who are in Christ Jesus."

Heavenly Father, thank you for desiring a relationship with me so intensely that you were willing to remove all the obstacles standing in the way. Give me the courage to ignore my feelings and take you at your word. By faith I choose to accept right now the fact that I am not condemned. In Jesus' name. Amen.

TOUCHSTONE

*In Christ we are completely
free from all condemnation.*

*In love he predestined us to be adopted
as his sons through Jesus Christ,
in accordance with his pleasure and will.*

Ephesians 1:5

How Free Is Free?

*T*here is all the difference in the world between working *to gain* someone's acceptance and working *because of* someone's acceptance. I meet people all the time who feel compelled to serve God in order to merit his love and acceptance. Often this is the result of a theological error they have been taught since childhood. "You better be good or else. . . ." On other occasions it stems from growing up in a home where parental acceptance depended on their behavior. "Be a good girl, and daddy will love you." This pattern of thinking can become so entrenched that adults will work themselves into the grave in an attempt to prove to their parents that they were not a failure. I have met men who were driven by a desire to gain their father's approval long after their father had passed away!

When this system of performance-based acceptance is transferred to our heavenly Father, the result is legalism. Legalism is an attitude. It is a system of thinking in which an individual attempts to gain God's love and acceptance through good works or service. Some people sincerely believe their salvation is at stake. For others it is a vague feeling of divine disapproval of which they are trying to rid themselves. Either way, however, legalism always leads to the same dead end: a lack of joy, a critical spirit, and an inability to be transparent.

Freedom from legalism comes through accepting the truth about our favored position in the family of God. Those who have put their trust in Christ have been *adopted* into his family. There is no concept that speaks any clearer of acceptance than adoption. Whereas a pregnancy can come as a surprise, adoption is always something that is premeditated and planned. While you and I were still without hope, God set the stage to adopt us into his family (Rom. 5:8).

Do you feel that you must work in order to gain God's acceptance? Do you find yourself being critical of those who do not serve the Lord with the same fervor as you? Have you

developed a martyr's attitude toward your service for the Lord? If you answered yes to any of these questions, it could be that you are not really resting in the finished work of Christ—a work that settled the question of your acceptability once and for all, a work that provided you with an eternal place in the family of God, a work that allows you to call the God of the universe your Father!

Heavenly Father, you are the God who overcame the barrier sin had put between us. Thank you for seeking me out and adopting me into your family. Thank you that I don't have to serve you in order to earn your love and acceptance. Remind me often of this liberating truth. Renew my mind so that I may serve you out of a heart of gratitude and joy. Amen.

TOUCHSTONE

*God's unconditional acceptance
sets us free to serve him
with unending joy.*

You intended to harm me,
but God intended it for good
to accomplish what is now being done. . . .
Genesis 50:20

Free to Believe

*T*rusting God to use the circumstantial disappointments in life is difficult. Trusting him to work through people's evil intentions is something else entirely. It is one thing when the church picnic is rained out. It is quite another when a "friend" at work intentionally lies in order to get your job.

When events such as a betrayal occur, a wall of frustration clouds our relationship with God. We ask, "Why didn't you stop this? Didn't you know this was going to happen?" As our frustration turns to doubt, we lose confidence in God's concern and involvement in our lives. After all, if he really has our best interest in mind, why would he allow us to suffer at the hands of our adversaries?

To be free from the doubt and resentment we tend to feel toward God when we are intentionally hurt by others, we must focus on the principle stated so clearly by Joseph: "You intended to harm me, but God intended it for good. . . ." Through all the rejection and abuse Joseph encountered at the hands of his brothers, God had not abandoned him. Just the opposite was true. Through the intentional mistreatment Joseph experienced, God was working to accomplish his divine plan.

There is a catch. In order for God to turn a negative situation into a positive one, we must remain faithful through the process. Imagine what would have happened if Joseph had allowed himself to grow bitter at God and at his family. This story may not have had such a happy ending. It was Joseph's faithfulness through the process that gave God the freedom to work.

Have you been mistreated? Has your faith in God's goodness and sovereignty been shaken? Are you willing to begin renewing your mind to the truth that what people may have intended for evil, God can use for your good and his glory?

Heavenly Father, you are the God who sovereignly uses even the intentional evil of human beings to carry out your will. Forgive me for harboring anger toward you for the wrongs done to me by others. I choose to believe that you are intimately aquainted with every detail of my life, that nothing goes unnoticed. Thank you for the assurance I have through Christ. I am excited to see how you will demonstrate your faithfulness in the days and weeks ahead. Amen.

TOUCHSTONE

The evil intentions of people, when responded to correctly, can become the very means by which God carries out his divine plans.

But immediately Jesus said to them:
"Take courage! It is I. Don't be afraid."
                                    Matthew 14:27

Fear Not!

*F*ear is probably the number-one cause of paralysis. By paralysis I do not mean some physical malady. The paralysis caused by fear affects the mind, will, and emotions. It is paralysis of the soul.

For years I have lived with the fear of being left alone. My father died when I was a baby. My mother worked in a mill while I was growing up. She had to leave for work while I was still asleep. It seemed as if I was always being left alone. As is always the case with unpleasant early experiences, mine also left their mark.

All of us have fears. Many have a fear of failure. Others struggle with a fear of commitment or of finding themselves trapped in a relationship. Occasionally I talk with a young person who fears growing old. And if we are honest, we have all felt a twinge of fear at the thought of dying.

As the disciples peered out across the windswept sea, they saw what they thought to be a ghost. The Scripture tells us that these brave, seasoned sailors actually "cried out" in fear (Matt. 14:26). Their fears were short-lived, however, for the next sound they heard was the voice of Jesus. And his presence alone brought peace to their hearts while the sea continued to rage around them.

Those who have placed their trust in Christ as Savior are never required to face either the known or the unknown alone; he is there. In those times when our fear surges from our knowledge of what is to come, he is there. He understands the terror that accompanies the prospect of severe pain, the loss of a loved one, or death. The Savior is no stranger to these. In times when it is the unknown that causes us to fear, he is there. He is there with full knowledge of what is to come and with the grace to sustain us.

Have your fears become a controlling force in your life? Do you find yourself missing opportunities and experiences because

of your fear of failure, rejection, or the future in general? God never intended for you to be controlled by fear. He is, however, willing to use your fears to move you to a place of greater dependence on him. Whatever it is you are facing, remember, he is there.

Heavenly Father, thank you for sending a Savior who can identify with my fears and who promised his presence in the midst of both the known and the unknown. Grant me the wisdom to draw upon his grace when I am overcome by fear. May my courage bring honor and glory to your name. Amen.

TOUCHSTONE

As you walk through the valley of the unknown, you will find the footprints of Jesus both in front of you and beside you.

Who is this uncircumcised Philistine
that he should defy the armies
of the living God?   1 Samuel 17:26

Overcoming Obstacles

*D*ay after day the army of Israel stood paralyzed with fear. However, it wasn't the size or strength of the Philistine army that terrified them. Israel had been outnumbered before. This time it was different. This time it was one soldier who stood between Israel and victory. Only one soldier. But he was no ordinary soldier. This was Goliath, the champion of the Philistine army—a warrior so intimidating to look upon that even his blasphemous taunts could not anger a single Israelite soldier to the point of being willing to confront him. To challenge Goliath would mean certain death. Or so it seemed.

Enter David. Upon seeing and hearing Goliath, the young shepherd asked a very insightful question—a question that introduced a fresh new perspective to the scene: "Who is this uncircumcised Philistine that he should defy the armies of the living God?"

Everyone saw the same towering figure in the valley. They all heard the same profanities. But David interpreted these things differently from those around him. Saul and his men saw Goliath as *their* enemy. David, on the other hand, saw Goliath as one coming against the living God. Take a moment and read David's speech beginning in 1 Samuel 17:45.

We all face Goliaths from time to time. Perhaps they are circumstances at work, relationships at home, or decisions just too big for us to handle. Like the soldiers of Israel, we are often overwhelmed with our own sense of inadequacy. So we stand motionless, lacking the courage to move ahead.

Freedom comes as we develop young David's attitude, when we adopt a heavenly perspective on all of life's obstacles. Because we are children of the living God, anything that comes against us must come through him. And in the words of the apostle Paul, "If God is for us, who can be against us?" (Rom. 8:31).

As you contemplate the challenges of today, don't make the mistake of measuring your potential success by your ability or

past performance. To do so means instant insecurity and discouragement. God gains much greater honor through our *availability* than through our *ability*. He does not expect you to work out the details of how everything is going to come together today. All he requires is that you show up and do what you believe he wants you to do, trusting him to fill in the gaps.

Heavenly Father, thank you for allowing me to face what seem to be impossible obstacles. These obstacles serve as a constant reminder of my intense dependence on you. Thank you as well for the promise of your strength and sufficiency. It is a great comfort to know I do not face Goliath alone. Father, I am available. I am trusting you to make me able. Amen.

TOUCHSTONE

God is not nearly so interested in your ability *as he is in your* availability.

Be kind and compassionate to one another,
forgiving each other,
just as in Christ God forgave you. Ephesians 4:32

Freedom to Forgive

*I*f you are like most people, you have been hurt at some time in your life. You may have suffered intense rejection as a child or at this very moment you may be in a relationship that results in a daily dose of hurt. Hurt, regardless of its intensity or longevity, sets each of us up to become a slave to resentment and bitterness. Our natural tendency is to hold on to the wrongs done to us by others. Without realizing it, we begin to view those who have offended us as owing us something. We begin expecting them to somehow pay us back for the emotional stress they have brought to our lives. Our desire to get even often results in fantasies of conversations we would like to have and plans we wish we had the nerve to carry out.

This is one of the most damaging types of bondage. I have watched men and women destroy those whom they loved the most because of their refusal to deal with resentment. Resentment is like a poisoned fountain. It pours out its poison into every relationship. Consequently, husbands, wives, children, and employees who had nothing to do with causing the hurt become its victims.

There is a way out. It is actually very simple. Forgive. "That's impossible," you say. Oh really? Think about it; what makes it impossible? Really only one thing, your refusal to let go of the lie that somehow those who have wronged you owe you something. To forgive is simply to mentally release the offending party of any obligation. "But," you say, "you don't know the pain and trouble they have caused me." That is true. But think about the pain and sorrow they are continuing to cause you by your refusal to let go. When you weigh the temporary joy you may experience when you contemplate revenge against the negative fallout in your relationships with others, is it worth it?

When it comes to forgiveness, Jesus set the standard. Meditate for a moment on this thought: *He who had the greatest reason not to forgive paid the highest price in order to forgive.* Jesus

died in order to make it *possible* for him to forgive you; and then, having paved the way, he *forgave* you. For us, forgiveness is simply a mental decision. For Christ, it was a matter of life and death. He chose death, in order that you may have life. Now then, if Christ was willing to release you from the debt you owed him, who are you to refuse to release those who have offended you? Besides, what do you have to gain by continuing to cling to your hurt? Why not let go of it right now?

Heavenly Father, you are the God who forgives. Thank you for forgiving me. Bring to my mind those wrongs I continue to cling to. Give me the strength and courage to forgive, as you have so graciously forgiven me. Amen.

TOUCHSTONE

*He who had the greatest
reason not to forgive paid
the highest price in order to
forgive.*

Then Peter came to Jesus and asked, "Lord, how many times shall I forgive my brother when he sins against me? Up to seven times?"
Jesus answered, "I tell you, not seven times, but seventy-seven times." Matthew 18:21–22

... and Forgive and Forgive and Forgive

*A*ll of us have been told at some time to *forgive and forget*. It sure sounds like a good idea, but unfortunately it is impossible to do. We do not have the ability to erase our memory banks. But wouldn't it be great if we could? Every time someone threw a hurtful remark your way, you could forgive that person and forget the wrong right there on the spot. The next time you saw him you wouldn't have anything to hold against him; it would have been forgotten. Such a system would make the forgiveness process so much easier. Forgiving someone for a one-time offense is not nearly so difficult as forgiving someone who is constantly hurting you. No doubt it was this very dilemma that drove Peter to ask Jesus how many times he should forgive his brother. Peter thought seven times was a gracious plenty. Jesus countered by suggesting seventy-seven times. From the parable that follows it is clear that Jesus really meant for Peter to forgive his brother every time he sinned against him—regardless of how often the occasion arose.

If you are like many people, there is someone in your life who hurts or offends you almost daily. It may be your unsaved spouse. It could be one of your children. For many it is an employee or an employer. Whatever the case, if there is someone like that in your life, you run a constant risk of becoming bitter. Simply forgiving such a person one time is not enough. You may literally have to forgive him seven times a day. In some extreme cases you may have to forgive him every time he opens his mouth!

I frequently talk to people who are harboring anger and resentment. When I raise the forgiveness issue, they will often respond by saying, "I have forgiven them, but they keep on hurting me!" Somewhere along the way these people got the idea

that once they forgive the offending party, that should be the end of it. But that is rarely the case. As long as an individual continues to offend, you must continue to forgive. That is, you must right there on the spot mentally release the offending person of any obligation. When I am in that kind of situation, I just smile and under my breath whisper, "Lord, I forgive her just as you forgave me."

The only way to stay free from resentment and bitterness is to get into the habit of forgiving immediately and unconditionally. Don't put it off. Delay gives the Enemy time to work on you. Think about it, how many times has God had to forgive you for the same sin? How many times has he had to forgive you for the same thing more than once on the same day? Follow his example—forgive and . . . well, just forgive.

Heavenly Father, you are the God whose forgiveness knows no boundaries. Just as you are constantly forgiving me, give me the wisdom to do the same for others. And in this way keep me free from the web of bitterness. Amen.

TOUCHSTONE

*Forgive completely,
immediately,* and
unconditionally.

And will not God bring about justice for his chosen ones, who cry out to him day and night? Will he keep putting them off?   *Luke 18:7*

Justice for All

We have all been treated unjustly at some time in our life. Our first impulse is to retaliate, to strike back, to work out a way to get even. To be honest, when I see people mistreated, I am often tempted to take revenge on their behalf. It is hard to sit by and watch others being taken advantage of—especially when it so often appears that the offending party goes unpunished.

The truth is that God is keeping good records of the injustice in this world. No evil act goes unnoticed. From snatched purses to lawsuits to abused children, he sees them all and takes careful notes. One day the last trumpet will sound and life as we know it will end. At that time the Judge of this world will set up court. Every crime since the beginning of time will be tried. And the amazing thing is that the Judge will also serve as an eyewitness to every case! When all is said and done, every man and woman will receive retribution of some kind for his or her deeds done on earth (2 Cor. 5:10).

The key to being set free from a desire to return evil for evil is to keep in mind two important truths. First, you are not the Judge, Christ is. He will return as the Judge of all mankind and dole out justice according to his infinite wisdom and knowledge. Second, the Son of God is still waiting to be avenged for the wrong done to him. As badly as you may have been mistreated, remember that Christ did not take revenge on those who crucified him. He reserved that for a future date. And so we wait. But we wait knowing that in the end all wrongs will be made right. And not one unjust act will have gone unnoticed.

Have you been treated unfairly? Are you guilty of attempting to get revenge through your words, your refusal to do your best for someone, or some other form of retribution? If so, are you now willing to turn that responsibility over to its rightful owner?

Heavenly Father, you are a God of justice—a God who allows no unjust deed to escape your notice. Thank you for the promise of retribution. Give us the courage to trust you. And grant us the self-control to wait. Amen.

TOUCHSTONE

*The day of judgment will be
a day of justice.*

What causes fights and quarrels among you? Don't they come from your desires that battle within you? You want something but don't get it. You kill and covet, but you cannot have what you want. You quarrel and fight.

James 4:1

When Rights Become Wrongs

*W*hat at first appears to be a serious case of oversimplification is actually a penetrating truth. All of our relational conflicts stem from our pursuit of pleasure or satisfaction. Since the fulfillment of our desires is often viewed as an infringement on the rights and fulfillment of others, there is conflict. And so husbands fight with their wives over where to spend their vacation. Employees and employers argue over wage increases. Neighbors argue over property lines. Think about your last confrontation. How did it begin? Isn't it true that it ultimately stemmed from someone's desire to have his or her own way?

When James speaks of desires, he is referring to every sort of desire—both good and evil. It is our desires that determine the arena for the conflicts we encounter. To make matters worse, we live in a society that exonerates those who know how to get their way. Yet it is that very characteristic that often serves as the basis for one's inability to get along with others.

As Christians we have been called to live beyond the world's standards. Specifically, we are not to live life consumed by having our way. Freedom from this treadmill pursuit of pleasure comes through the most basic of all Christian principles—trust. When it appears that your needs are about to go unmet and that your desires are going to go unfulfilled, your response must be, "Lord, I trust you." To do otherwise is to set yourself up for conflict. The apostle Paul knew what it was like to go without. Drawing from the wealth of his own experience, he encouraged a group of needy believers with these words: "My God will meet all your needs according to his glorious riches in Christ Jesus" (Phil. 4:19).

What is the source of your quarrels? God says that ultimately

it is your determination to have your way. Today begin surrendering your rights and desires to the One who has promised to meet your every need. One practical way is to write down the areas of conflict in your life. Beside each one write down the right or desire that contributes to your run-ins. One by one surrender those to God. Then place your list in an envelope and put it somewhere as a reminder that you are trusting God to meet your every need—his way and in his time.

Heavenly Father, you are the God who is intimately acquainted with my every need and desire. Thank you for concerning yourself with the details of my life. Thank you for the example I have in Christ, who willingly laid down his rights—even his right to life itself. Give me the courage to trust you when others prove insensitive and untrustworthy. Amen.

TOUCHSTONE

Life's conflicts diminish as we surrender our rights and desires to Christ.

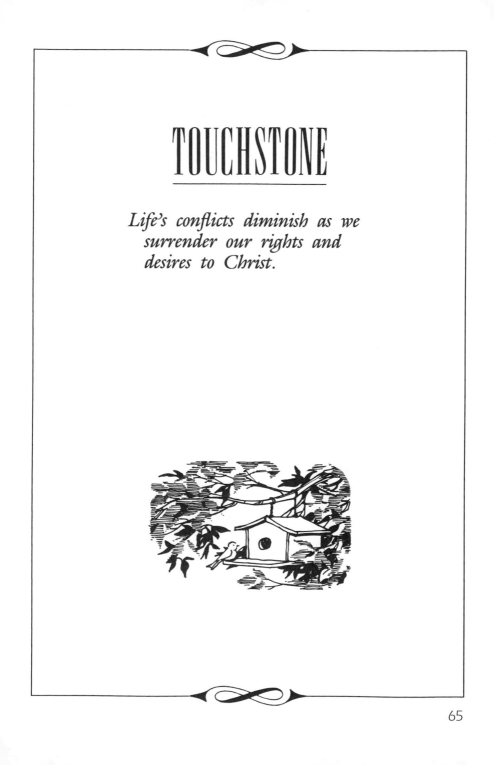

Let us then approach the throne of grace
     with confidence,
so that we may receive mercy and find grace
to help us in our time of need.   *Hebrews 4:16*

Great Expectations

*A*nyone who has experienced the frustration of unanswered prayer knows what it is like to be disappointed with God. When he does not respond the way we expect him to, we immediately begin searching for the reason. The age-old questions concerning God and evil begin to whirl through our minds: "If God is a good God why would he allow. . . ? If God is all powerful, surely he could have stopped. . . ." And each round of questions steadily chips away at our confidence. For many, this process leads to total hopelessness and despair. For others, it culminates in faith so crippled that this faith becomes virtually useless.

I too have been disappointed with God. My experiences have brought me to these two conclusions: (1) God always keeps his promises, but (2) we are not always careful to claim just his promises. Often we confuse what he has promised with what we wish, desire, and hope for. Consequently, our faith becomes focused on the fulfillment of things God never intended to do. And we are disappointed.

Nowhere in Scripture does God promise to fine-tune our circumstances to our liking. Nowhere does he guarantee a pain-free, problem-free environment. As his children we are free to ask for whatever our hearts desire. But as his servants we must submit ourselves to his sovereign will.

There are, however, two promised gifts we can claim with absolute confidence—mercy and grace. The Savior can sympathize with you. He knows from experience what it means to suffer alone. When you cry out to him, he moves to the edge of his throne to listen attentively and compassionately. You hold a tender place in his heart.

But he does more than listen. Jesus personally extends to us the strength we need to endure whatever it is we are facing. That is the idea behind the term *grace*.

The heavenly Father may elect not to change the nature of

your circumstances. He may in fact choose to deliver you *through* hard times rather than *from* them. His answer to your prayers of deliverance may be "Hang in there!" But this is no time for disappointment. God is not ignoring your cry for help; he is extending to you the power to withstand whatever difficulty or pain life brings your way. And he does so in the hope that having withstood it, you will one day stand and give him all the glory!

Heavenly Father, thank you for not turning a deaf ear to the cries of your children. Father, I confess that I have been disappointed with what has seemed to be a lack of concern on your part. I realize now that I was holding you to promises you never made. As I face the difficulties of life I do so with the confidence that you listen to my cries compassionately and that you will always provide me with the strength to endure. Amen.

TOUCHSTONE

When you come to the Father,
you will always find mercy
and grace in time of need.

Who are you to judge someone else's servant?
To his own master he stands or falls.
And he will stand. . . . Romans 14:4

Agree to Disagree

*T*here are issues on which the church of the Lord Jesus will never come to full agreement. The apostle Paul coined the term "disputable matters" when referring to these types of things. In his day the hot topic was eating meat offered to idols or not eating meat at all. Today believers debate over things such as clapping in church, music, dancing, hair style, drinking wine, and the proper form of church government.

As important as these things may be, God never intended for them to divide the church. Yet it is amazing how they cause believers to become highly critical of one another. This attitude results in gossip, slander, divisiveness, and many other evils that the Scripture clearly teaches are wrong (Eph. 4:29–32). Those who involve themselves in this type of criticism are good examples of what Jesus was referring to when he said, "Why do you look at the speck of sawdust in your brother's eye and pay no attention to the plank in your own eye?" (Matt. 7:3)

The truth that sets us free from a critical spirit is found in Romans 14. Paul makes it penetratingly clear that we have no right to judge someone else's servant. What he is referring to is the fact that each of us is a servant of Christ. And the time will come when each of us will give an account of our life to him— the One to whom we are ultimately accountable. When it comes to disputable matters, we were never appointed to be one another's judge. We are free to disagree, but we are never free to criticize. To judge others for their opinion on "disputable matters" is to take upon ourselves a role God reserves exclusively for his Son.

Do you find yourself criticizing other believers for things that are really matters of opinion rather than clear moral or ethical issues? Do you tend to judge others' spirituality, based on trivial things? Are you guilty of taking upon yourself the role of judge?

Heavenly Father, you are the judge of the living and the dead. You are the God who is able to see beyond a person's actions and take into account the motivation of his heart. I am grateful that you have reserved for yourself the role of judge. Thank you for not setting me as a judge over my brothers and sisters in Christ in the area of disputable matters. Please convict me when I become critical and thus take upon myself a responsibility you never intended for me. Thank you for the freedom and diversity that there is in the body of Christ. Amen.

TOUCHSTONE

*To our own Master we will
stand or fall.*

And I hope that, as you have understood us in part,
you will come to understand fully
that you can boast of us just as we will boast of you
in the day of the Lord Jesus.   2 Corinthians 1:14

Beyond Behavior

*W*e all know people we don't like. It's the guy you pretend not to see as he waves to you across the parking lot. It's the "old friend" whose calls your secretary knows not to put through to your office. It's the self-styled theologian who always wants to talk to you after church. It's an employee, an employer, a neighbor, a relative. . . . The list goes on and on. They are everywhere.

I know, I know—Christians are supposed to love everybody. That may be true. But *love* is one thing, *like* is something else altogether. We can force ourselves to be kind and patient and gentle and all of that. But how do you make yourself *like* someone?

To overcome our dislike for people we must first understand a little bit about what makes them tick. Folks are not generally born unlikable. They get that way with time and abuse. As we begin to understand the person behind the behavior, some of the walls begin to come down.

God used an event several summers ago to remind me once again of this simple yet profound principle. The incident took place at a family-life conference where I was the keynote speaker. Early in the week I had my first encounter with Jimmy. Actually, I heard him before I saw him. We were just about to begin a session when a raspy voice could be heard practically screaming, "Excuse me. Excuse me." Through a crowd came this little boy, dragging a chair behind him. After almost knocking down several attendees, he made his way to the front, crammed his chair between two other chairs—both of which were occupied— and sat down. He looked around for a second, stood up, and started yelling back over the crowd, "Mom, Mom, there's a seat up here!" My first impulse was to snatch him up and tan his hide. By mid-week everybody knew Jimmy—and shared my sentiments.

Then something interesting happened. A woman at the

conference pulled me over to the side to tell me something in private. She asked if I had met Jimmy yet. I smiled and assured her I had. She explained how she had befriended him early in the week and that they had been talking together. She continued, "This morning Jimmy walked up and said he had something he wanted to tell me. I asked him what it was. Without hesitation he said, 'My daddy dropped dead in January, and I'm having a hard time.'" When I heard that, my feelings for Jimmy immediately changed. I wanted to find him and hug him. Now I understood.

Who is it that just drives you crazy? You will be free from many of your negative feelings when you discover the truth about the person behind the behavior.

Heavenly Father, thank you for looking beyond my behavior and loving me anyway. Grant me the wisdom and the courage to do the same for others. As I encounter those whose company I don't particularly enjoy, remind me to look at the person behind the behavior. Amen.

TOUCHSTONE

*Take time to look at the
person behind the behavior.*

*I tell you, use worldly wealth to gain friends
for yourselves, so that when it is gone,
you will be welcomed into eternal dwellings.*

Luke 16:9

Financial Freedom

*E*ven a casual look around is enough to confirm the truth of these words that Paul wrote to Timothy: "The love of money is a root of all kinds of evil" (1 Tim. 6:10). Volumes could be written on the ways this truth has worked its way into the lives of unsuspecting men and women. Every crime has at some time been motivated by somebody's all-consuming desire for money. On a more personal level, the love of money has been the wedge used to alienate husbands from wives, fathers from sons, and even best friends from each other. The greatest tragedies, however, are those in which a man or woman's love for money has caused him or her to drift away from Christ.

What makes this such a tough issue is that it is difficult to discern whether or not we are victims of this dreaded infirmity. How can we tell if we are lovers of money? Rather than give us a list of things by which to evaluate ourselves, Jesus offered us a new perspective on the whole issue of our finances. The implication is that if we will adopt his attitude toward money, we will never have to worry about its becoming the object of our affection.

For some, money is an end in itself. Christ viewed it as a means to an end. Specifically, he viewed it as *a temporal means to an eternal end.* God views every dollar we possess as well as all our material possessions as tools—tools to be used with the express purpose of bringing people into his kingdom. Take a minute and read Jesus' parable in Luke 16. Take careful note of verse 9. Jesus said that when we enter heaven, we will be greeted by those whose salvation was secured by our giving. Every dollar you send to missions that is instrumental in someone's coming to Christ will add one more person to your welcoming party.

When you think about your money, you are to think of it in this light: "How can I use what I own to more effectively reach people for Christ?" To the degree that you adopt this attitude

toward your money and possessions, you will be free from the love of money.

Heavenly Father, you are the God who takes what is temporal and uses it to bring yourself eternal glory. Thank you for those who gave of their time and energy and possessions to provide me with an opportunity to hear the gospel. Remind me of this truth daily. And in doing so, protect me from setting my affection on the accumulation of wealth. Amen.

TOUCHSTONE

Money is a means, not an end—a tool to provide people with opportunities to hear and accept the gospel of Christ.

When they came to the border of Mysia,
they tried to enter Bithynia,
but the Spirit of Jesus would not allow them to.
Acts 16:7 (cf. Jeremiah 29:11)

Future Frustrations

O ne of the most common questions I am asked is, "How can I know God's will for my life?" Many times there is a great deal of anxiety in the voice of the one asking. Understandably so. It is discouraging when we don't know what direction God wants us to take.

It is unfortunate that so many Christians are paralyzed by the question of God's will. Many feel that until they know absolutely, beyond a shadow of a doubt, exactly what God wants them to do, they don't dare to make a move. But that is not the model we find in Scripture. In fact just the opposite is true.

Paul is a good example. He knew God's general will for his life—that he should preach the gospel. So he took off to do just that. The implication of what happened in Acts 16 is that Paul did not always get specific direction from the Lord. And when he didn't, he simply did what he thought was best for him to do. Apparently Paul heard that Bithynia needed the gospel; so he headed out in that direction. But God had another plan for Paul and blocked the way.

If you don't know God's specific will for your life, chances are it is because he has not revealed it to you. In the meantime you are free to begin moving in whatever direction you feel is appropriate. If you make a wrong choice, God will stop you just as he stopped the apostle Paul. God never intended for us to be paralyzed by his silence. There is enough general guidance in his Word to get us on our way. As long as we are unsure of the specifics in life, we are free to make what we consider the best decision to be—again, knowing that he can step in at any time and change our direction.

Has your search for the "perfect" will of God left you in a holding pattern? Maybe it's time to make a move. Don't be afraid to do what you feel is best. For within the plan God has designed for each of us, he has included a measure of freedom as well.

Heavenly Father, you are the God who knows my fears and frustrations concerning the future. I confess that often I get anxious about your timing. Beginning today I am choosing to trust you to reveal everything I need to know at the perfect time. For now I will do what I feel is best. Through this process I am trusting you to stop me should I begin to move in the wrong direction or in the right direction at the wrong time. Thank you for the freedom to think and decide for myself as well as for your promise of guidance. Lead me to a perfect balance of the two. Amen.

TOUCHSTONE

*Included in God's will for
your life is the freedom to
explore and pursue the
desires of your heart.*

Let us not become weary in doing good,
for at the proper time we will reap a harvest
if we do not give up.   Galatians 6:9

Dealing With Discouragement

*E*veryone enjoys immediate results. Whether it is a salesman making calls, a grandmother planting a garden, or a college graduate sending out resumés—no one enjoys waiting. This same tendency carries over into our spiritual lives as well. Once we commit a situation to the Lord, we expect things to change—*now!* If we are convicted of a particular sin in our lives and turn to our heavenly Father for help, we want to experience instantaneous freedom. When we become burdened for someone and begin praying on that person's behalf, we expect God to do something soon.

But often nothing happens. Our prayers go unanswered, and our effort goes unrewarded. It is during these times that we are most prone to get discouraged. Our confidence in the faithfulness of God wanes. We may even entertain doubts about his very existence.

For many people discouragement is the first stage in a multitude of emotionally crippling disorders. For others it serves as the catalyst for their theological pilgrimage—a pilgrimage that more often than not leads them to conclusions contrary to that of Scripture.

Discouragement is not part of God's plan for his children. To be free—and to remain free—from discouragement we must spiritually digest the promise in Galatians 6:9 to the point that it becomes a part of our thinking. To paraphrase the apostle Paul, it pays to do good. We may not see any immediate results from our good works, but the Scripture clearly teaches that God is taking notes (e.g., Mal. 3:14–16). At the proper time our faithfulness will be rewarded.

The tension centers around God's timing. We want results now. But in many cases God chooses to wait. The first step in

digging our way out of the pit of discouragement is to decide once and for all whether or not we are willing to live according to God's timetable. If not, discouragement will become a way of life. But once we entrust ourselves to his care—which of course includes his timing—we have hope; the one thing a discouraged man or woman has little or none of.

Are you discouraged? Does it seem that you are laboring in vain? Take a few moments to meditate on Galatians 6:9. Ask God to restore your confidence in him and his timetable for your life. And rest assured that you will in fact reap a good harvest, if you refuse to give up!

Heavenly Father, you are a God who rewards your faithful servants. You see and take note of all my labor. Thank you for the illustration of this that you have given us through your Son, who was greatly rewarded for his work on earth. Grant me the courage and endurance to keep on keeping on so that I may reap a reward at the proper time. Amen.

TOUCHSTONE

Persistence pays.

Do not be anxious about anything,
but in everything, by prayer and petition,
with thanksgiving, present your requests to God.
                                            Philippians 4:6

Worry

*T*here are places in Scripture where it appears that the writer is guilty of oversimplification. The way some topics are handled makes me wonder if the author has any idea of the type of world we live in. Paul's statement in Philippians 4:6 is one of those passages. How can he say, with such apparent flippancy, "Do not be anxious about anything"? Maybe you are tempted to respond to this verse the way I used to: "Paul, if you had my schedule, my financial obligations, and my responsibilities at home you would change your tune. Anybody who believes we should never worry has never really had anything to worry about."

As impractical as the advice in this verse may seem, there is one thing that brings me back to it again and again: Paul was in prison when he penned these words. Furthermore, Paul was a man consumed with a desire to take the Gospel of Christ all over the world. He was not somebody who enjoyed sitting around—much less sitting around chained to a Roman soldier. Yet in the midst of these far-less-than-ideal surroundings we find him admonishing the Christians in Philippi not to worry.

This brings us to some important questions: "What did Paul know that we don't know? How could he manage not to worry when his life and everything he had worked and lived for appeared to be in jeopardy?" He tells us in the second half of the verse: "But in everything, by prayer and petition, with thanksgiving, present your requests to God."

Paul trusted God completely. *He replaced worry with prayer, anxiety with faith.* He had a habit of remembering what we so easily forget—God is in control, and nothing takes him by surprise. God knew where Paul was. And he knew what Paul was and wasn't getting done. That was enough for the apostle. And the fact that he knows all about us must be enough for us as well.

What are you worried about? Try this: every time you begin to worry, pray instead. Tell the Lord what's going on and what

you feel needs to go on. Give him the details—your fears, your dreams, everything. Then tell him that unless he comes through, you are in trouble. In other words, put the burden on his shoulders. When you begin to worry again, repeat the process. After a couple of rounds of prayer you will begin experiencing peace. Long before your circumstances change, your feelings will change; you will sense a new internal freedom. Faith always brings freedom. What are you worrying about? Pray.

Heavenly Father, you are the God who knows my every care. You know the demands of this day. You are even aware of the added burdens tomorrow will bring. Remind me, Father, that you never intended for me to carry even one day's cares alone but that you have made yourself available to share and sometimes even bear my load. Remind me to pray rather than worry. Replace my anxiety with faith. Amen.

TOUCHSTONE

*Replace worry with prayer,
and anxiety with faith.*

Do nothing out of selfish ambition or vain conceit, but in humility consider others better than yourselves. Each of you should look not only to his own interests, but also to the interests of others. Your attitude should be the same as that of Christ Jesus.   Philippians 2:3–5

Controlling Conceit

No one enjoys being around individuals who are eaten up with themselves—men and women who are always talking about where *they* have been, who *they* know, and what *they* have accomplished. Although we can spot conceit in others a mile away, it is usually difficult to recognize it in ourselves. This is compounded by the fact that conceit takes on so many different forms. It's not only the loudmouth who can't stop talking about his or her last "big deal" who suffers from a case of conceit. Often it is the guy who never says a word—the one who is so absorbed in his own affairs that he can't be bothered by the concerns of others. The many disguises of conceit make each of us a vulnerable target.

In order to keep ourselves free from the web of conceit we must continually strive for humility. Maybe the idea of *striving for humility* sounds like a contradiction in terms. Perhaps, like many folks, you have always thought humility is just something some people are born with. Not so. Humility is something that is developed. In fact, we must all actively pursue humility or we will slowly gravitate toward some form of conceit.

So how do we free ourselves from conceit? How do we become humble? It is really very simple. Think of someone you admire, maybe someone you have admired from a distance but have never met. Choose someone who in the broad scheme of things you would consider *better* than you. Okay? How would you treat this individual if he or she were the next person you were to come into contact with? Now, make a decision to treat the next person you come into contact with the way you would the one you consider better than you. That is the *attitude* of humility. "But," you say, "what if I don't really believe the next person I come into contact with is better than I?" It doesn't matter! Just consider him to be better. That is the key to humility. It begins with an attitude.

There is one more thing. Make a decision to focus your next

conversation on the interests of the one you are talking with rather than your own. That is the *action* of humility. Ask questions. Listen attentively.

Jesus Christ did not die for you because you were actually worth dying for. He died for you because he *considered* you worth dying for. He put your best interests above his own—and he willingly marched to Calvary. Are you ready to be free from conceit? Then begin right now by preparing for your next encounter.

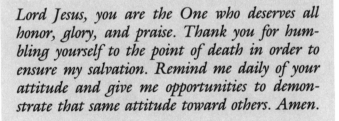

Lord Jesus, you are the One who deserves all honor, glory, and praise. Thank you for humbling yourself to the point of death in order to ensure my salvation. Remind me daily of your attitude and give me opportunities to demonstrate that same attitude toward others. Amen.

TOUCHSTONE

Consider others better, more worthy, and more honorable than yourself.

God said to him, "You fool!
This very night your life will be demanded from you.
Then who will get what you have prepared for
yourself?" Luke 12:20

Guarding Against Greed

I have never met a greedy man in my life. What I mean is that I have never met a person who would characterize himself or herself as greedy. Although greed is not a difficult term to define, it is terribly difficult to spot—in ourselves, that is. As one man put it, "The greedy man is the man who is more concerned about the accumulation of possessions than I am."

Greed creeps up on us. It begins with a sincere pursuit of fairness, a desire for our portion of the pie. Then somewhere along the way our campaign for fairness becomes a tool to justify irresponsible spending and accumulation. We defend our practice by reasoning that since it is *our* money we have the right to spend it as we please.

Jesus had some stern words for the greedy of his day. Take a minute and read Luke 12:13–34. No doubt the rich man in Jesus' parable was admired by those who knew him—just as we have a tendency to admire those who accumulate large fortunes today. But God called him a fool. "Now wait," we think; "maybe he was a little selfish, but a fool? How can a man who has the know-how to accumulate such incredible wealth be a fool?" Notice too that there is no mention of any wrongdoing on his part. Apparently he *earned* every penny of his massive estate. Yet God called him a fool. Why?

This man who was so wise in the things of this world was ignorant of the things of God. In his frenzy to accumulate wealth in this life he forgot about life in the hereafter. His mistake cost him dearly and eternally. Just as he was positioning himself for a life of ease, comfort, and pleasure, he lost it all. The very thing he refused to do willingly—give—he was ultimately forced to do.

Jesus went right to the heart of the matter when he said, "So is the man who lays up treasure for himself, and is not rich

toward God" (Luke 12:21). That is God's definition of greed: the pursuit of things here with little or no regard for the kingdom of God.

What percentage of your income do you invest in the kingdom of God? According to Jesus' definition, are you greedy? The truth that will set you free is this: on the day you die you will automatically give away all you own, but you will receive no credit for it in heaven. You have a choice. You can begin giving it away now—and have an unfailing treasure in heaven. Or you can continue to accumulate for yourself treasures on earth and have them taken from you by force. The choice is yours. The choice is clear.

Heavenly Father, you have set the precedent by giving your Son. Use this truth to revolutionize both my spending and my giving habits. I want to be rich toward you. Remind me to be on guard against greed. Give me discernment to catch it in its early stages and the courage to make whatever changes are necessary. Amen.

TOUCHSTONE

*Each of us will eventually
give away all our earthly
possessions. How we choose to
do so, however, is a
reflection of our commitment
to the kingdom of God.*

We must pay more careful attention,
therefore, to what we have heard,
so that we do not drift away. Hebrews 2:1

The Danger of Drifting

*D*uring the Second World War a battleship was anchored at the Azores off the coast of Spain. The sailors on watch asked a group of infantry men who happened to go on board, to stand watch while they went below for a meal. The soldiers were more than willing to help.

Unfortunately, they were untrained for their new responsibility. They were unaware that the ship's anchor was not secure and that the ship was gradually drifting toward shallow water. A trained seaman knows that he must periodically check a stationary landmark to keep tabs on the stability of a ship's anchorage. These eager soldiers, however, had not been taught what to watch for.

Within an hour the ship had drifted against a line of rocks. Minutes later a wave lifted the ship onto the rocks, ripping a hole in the bow. An alarm sounded, and the ship was evacuated. As the big cruiser heaved to one side, some equipment on deck collided and caught fire. Soon the entire vessel was engulfed in flames.

There is an unseen current that we all battle every day—a current that leads to certain destruction. We have all seen people drift away from God and the things of God. Oftentimes these are people we considered strong Christians.

Whenever I hear about something like that or see it happen, I always think about two things. First, everybody is susceptible; and I am certainly no exception. Second, I think about the warning in Hebrews 2:1. Here the author gives us the key to staying free from the effects of the tide that is constantly working to move us away from fellowship with the Father. "Pay attention!" he says. That is, "Direct your focus to the things pertaining to Christ and salvation." *We have a tendency to drift*

toward that on which we have focused our attention. This is why the Enemy is constantly working to get our attention—so he can influence our life's direction.

In light of how you spend your time and money, what is your focus? What are you paying close attention to during this time of your life? Has something or someone other than Christ captured your attention? If so, chances are you have begun to drift.

If the soldiers on deck had been paying attention to the shore in order to check the ship's movement, they could have avoided disaster. If you develop the habit of paying attention to a few reference points in your spiritual life, you too can avoid the eventual disaster that accompanies drifting.

Heavenly Father, thank you for this warning. Thank you for your concern. Give me keen insight into my own spiritual life so that I may catch myself in the initial stages of the process of drifting away from you. Make me a person whose focus is on Christ, and Christ alone. Amen.

TOUCHSTONE

The focus of our attention will determine our life's direction.

Every good and perfect gift is from above,
coming down from the Father of the heavenly lights. . .
James 1:17

A Grateful Heart

*T*he more I have, the more difficult it becomes to ward off ingratitude. As a child I was grateful for even the smallest blessing. My father died when I was only seven months old. My mother was left with almost nothing. By the time I was seventeen years old, I had lived in sixteen different houses in the same town. Gratitude came easy in those days. We were doing our best to survive. Every penny was counted and appreciated.

I guess one way to overcome an ungrateful spirit would be to lose everything. The old adage is true, you never know what you've got till it's gone. Anyone who has gone through a bankruptcy or been sued to the point of financial ruin can tell you all about that.

Other than by losing everything, how can we be free from ingratitude? Surely there is a way, for we are commanded to "give thanks in all circumstances" (1 Thess. 5:18).

To begin with, we must deal with an attitude that most of us adhere to in some form or another. It's an attitude that assumes we deserve the good life, that our hard work or perhaps the quality of our character has earned for us certain blessings and rewards. The truth, however, is that we deserve nothing. Why? Because sin separated us from the One who is the creator and bestower of all good things. It is only by the grace of God as expressed in Christ that we are allowed to participate in any good thing. Apart from God's love and concern for his prized creation there would be a vast chasm between us and all that is good in life.

There is no room for ingratitude in the life of a believer. For the truth is that *every* good gift is a grace gift from our heavenly Father. Why not take a few moments right now and thank him for the good things?

Heavenly Father, thank you for not giving me what I really deserve. I recognize that every good thing in my life is a grace gift from you. Guard me from the lie that somehow I deserve the good things in life. Remind me to express my gratitude daily—even for the smallest blessings. Thank you most of all for the gift of Jesus Christ. Amen.

TOUCHSTONE

Every good thing is from above.

*Do not let this Book of the Law depart
   from your mouth;
meditate on it day and night, so that you may be careful
to do everything written in it.
Then you will be prosperous and successful.   Joshua 1:8*

Free to Succeed

Next time you see a professional juggler, pay attention to where he focuses his attention. One would think a juggler would look at his hands, since that is where all the action is taking place. But a good juggler rarely looks down at his hands. He focuses on the point at which the objects he is juggling stop ascending and begin their descent. However, he does not watch any one object. He keeps his focus on the highest point.

Like the juggler, each of us has a number of things we must keep in motion—job, marriage, church, ministries, hobbies, children, education, etc. Our tendency is to begin focusing on one item to the neglect of others. We are deceived into believing that success in one area is an indication that we are successful, overall; when all the while we may be failing miserably in other departments. I have seen very talented women become so involved in social concerns that they fail in their responsibilities at home. We all know men whose financial accomplishments are the only measure of success they take seriously.

A juggler who could successfully juggle only one pin would not be considered much of a success. And a man or woman whose focus in life is any one area to the exclusion of the others is not much of a success either. Yet this is the situation in which many well-meaning believers find themselves.

The truth by which we can be set free from this dilemma is this: God will make you successful as you focus your attention on remaining faithful. God is committed to making you successful. The principles in his Word were given for that very purpose. But God takes a holistic approach. His goal is to grant you success in every area. He wants all your pins to stay airborne. The moment our focus becomes success rather than faithfulness, we begin working against God. At best we will be successfully juggling one pin while the others lie in disarray around us.

What is your focus, success or faithfulness? If it is difficult for you to imagine allowing God to prosper you at his pace

rather than your own and if the idea of shifting your focus away from success and onto faithfulness is a little threatening, think about the alternatives. Think about the price you are paying. Take a look at the lives of those who have traveled this road before you. Look at their health, their families, their reputation, their friends. Is it time you reevaluated the real meaning of success?

Father, you are the perfect picture of success. You keep all things perfectly balanced and in order. Give me the courage to turn my attention away from those things by which I tend to measure my success and to focus my eyes on you. Beginning today, I trust you to prosper me your way and according to your timetable.

TOUCHSTONE

Focus on faithfulness and trust God to make you successful.

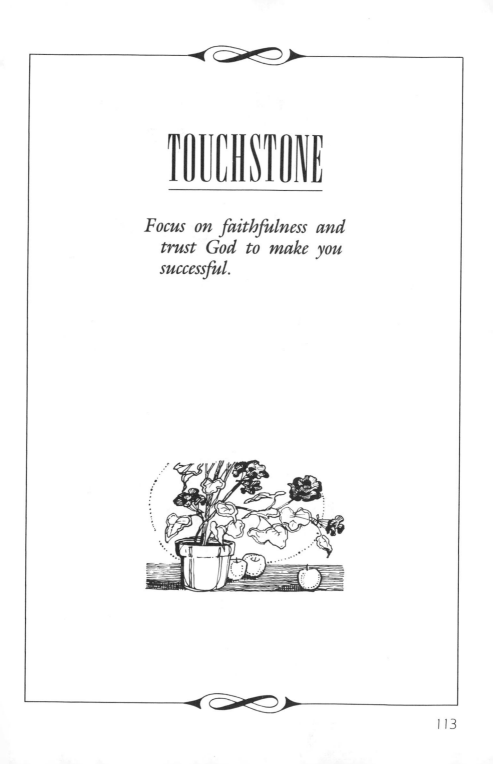

Be still and know that I am God.   Psalm 46:10

A New Orientation

I am a textbook example of a goal-oriented, achievement-directed, bottom-line individual. Anyone who is like that or lives with someone like that knows both the positives and negatives associated with this kind of personality. One of the negatives is that it is difficult for me to slow down and relax. Even worse, sometimes it is difficult for me to pull away from my to-do list and focus on the One for whom I am supposedly to-doing!

There are several things that contribute to this problem. One is the value system of the world we live in. The world does not reward those whose character is beyond reproach. Neither does it recognize those who have a growing knowledge of God. Consequently, we are prone to begin measuring our success by the world's definition—visible achievement and progress. It should go without saying that there is nothing wrong with achievement and progress. However, when these things become our primary focus, it is only a matter of time until our private lives will begin to crumble from abuse and neglect.

I believe with all my heart that it is impossible to be both goal-oriented and God-oriented at the same time. One orientation will always take precedence over the other. Jesus said it this way: "No servant can serve two masters. Either he will hate the one and love the other, or he will be devoted to the one and despise the other" (Luke 16:13). When our desire to achieve takes the lead, several things happen in our relationship with God. He becomes a means to an end rather than the end. We tend to use God rather than worship him. We will find ourselves seeking *information about* him rather than *transformation by* him.

The question remains: How do we free ourselves from an unhealthy dose of goal orientation and become God-oriented? David summed it up beautifully: "Be still, and know that I am God." That is, *stop* whatever you are doing. Turn on the answering machine, turn down the volume, turn off the

television, put down the paper, close your door, and think. Item by item think about the things that absorb your time, emotion, and energy. Now measure their importance by this one single truth: "He is God."

So you have deadlines—He is God. Your kids are sick—He is God. Your boss is coming down hard on you—He is God. Your marriage is at an all-time low—He is God. David's point is simple. Take all that concerns you and measure it by this one overarching truth. And, suddenly, your focus shifts. Nothing is quite as monumental as you had thought. Circumstances are not quite as overwhelming. Things begin to settle into their proper perspective. After all, He is God.

This renewal of perspective is not a quarterly review of your life. There are days when it needs to be an hourly exercise. Regardless of your circumstances, take time every day to stop and reflect on all of life's demands in light of the One who sovereignly and lovingly watches over you at all times.

Heavenly Father, you are the God who never sleeps or slumbers. You are the Master of all creation. You are the standard by which all things are measured. Remind me to approach all of life mindful of the fact that you are God. Amen.

TOUCHSTONE

It is impossible to be both goal-oriented and God-oriented at the same time.

For even the Son of Man did not come to be served,
but to serve, and to give his life as a ransom for many.
Mark 10:45

The Service Syndrome

*W*e live in a service-oriented society. Every year the demand for services increases. You can hire someone to do just about anything. Businesses designed to meet this growing demand are cropping up everywhere. Nowadays you can have just about any type of food brought to your home. Catalog companies have made it possible to purchase everything from clothes to camping gear by phone. You can even punch a few keys on your PC and have your groceries delivered right to your front door.

All of us enjoy being served. Isn't it true that a significant portion of our personal budgets go toward paying for services: water, electricity, housekeeping, babysitting, lawn care, interest payments, car repair, etc.? Many of these services are luxuries we have grown so accustomed to having that we consider them necessities.

With so much available to us we are set up to believe a lie that has been around since Jesus' day. Simply put, it is this: *Those who are served the most, are the most important.* Or, the greatest of all are served by all. We need to learn on a spiritual level what many businesses are learning on a monetary level. It is really those who do the serving who reap the most benefit. In this world, the businesses that can offer the greatest number of services to their customers will win the lion's share of the market; they will reap the greatest reward. Similarly, the believer who is the greatest servant in this life will reap the greatest reward in the life to come.

We are rulers in training. To be great later on in God's kingdom, you and I must be servants now. This runs against our grain for two reasons. First of all because the world has modeled the opposite for us all our lives. And second, our sinful flesh is constantly crying out for recognition and service. Regardless of the resistance we face, however, we would be wise to begin practicing servanthood today; it is the key to greatness in the kingdom to come.

As you think through the day ahead, who are the people you normally expect to serve you? How could you serve them instead? "For even the Son of Man did not come to be served, but to serve, and to give his life as a ransom for many."

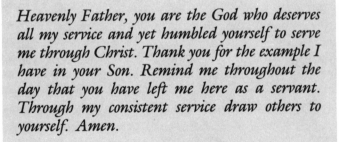

Heavenly Father, you are the God who deserves all my service and yet humbled yourself to serve me through Christ. Thank you for the example I have in your Son. Remind me throughout the day that you have left me here as a servant. Through my consistent service draw others to yourself. Amen.

TOUCHSTONE

*Those who serve in this life
will rule in the world to
come.*

Then he said to them all:
"If anyone would come after me,
he must deny himself
and take up his cross daily and follow me."

Luke 9:23

The Risk of Surrender

To the nonbeliever the idea of unconditionally surrendering oneself to a God no one can see sounds ludicrous. Understandably so. But even to many seasoned Christians the notion of surrender is somewhat threatening. Something on the inside of each of us shrinks back at the thought of abandoning ourselves to do God's bidding. As much as we enjoy singing about his sacrifice for us, the thought of returning the favor—unconditionally—makes us a little antsy.

When Jesus spoke of denying ourselves he was not thinking of some sort of monastic existence. Jesus did not live his life hidden away from the world. To deny ourselves is to simply say no to our desires when they conflict with God's will. Jesus made it clear that he did not have a single act in mind. He was calling for a lifestyle of denial. In another words, *sacrifice*.

Maybe the very thought of such a thing makes you shudder. You are not alone. Churches are full of people who need to be set free from their fear of sacrifice. And there is a simple truth that will do just that.

In the verses that follow today's passage Jesus mentions three things that will take place in the lives of those who refuse to follow him. In essence he is saying, "I understand what you are feeling. I understand your fear of the unknown. But take a good look at the alternatives, and you will understand why following me is the wisest choice you could make."

What are the alternatives? First of all, the people who can't find it within themselves to live for Christ will eventually lose everything they have lived for anyway. There will be nothing of eternal value to show for their lives. It's true, you can't take it with you. Second, those who see sacrifice for Christ as a threat to their security will eventually lose everything they thought made them secure to begin with. In essence, they will lose themselves. And last, refusing to surrender to the lordship of Christ results in the forfeiting of eternal status and recognition. Jesus put it this

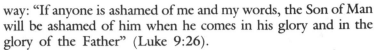

way: "If anyone is ashamed of me and my words, the Son of Man will be ashamed of him when he comes in his glory and in the glory of the Father" (Luke 9:26).

When you think about it, the man or woman who refuses to surrender to the will of God is really the one making the greatest sacrifice. Jim Elliott had it right when he said, "He is no fool who gives what he cannot keep to gain what he cannot lose." Have you been holding out on God? What is it that he wants from you? In light of eternity, is it really that much of a sacrifice? In light of eternity, is it really a sacrifice at all?

Heavenly Father, thank you for sacrificing what was most precious to you in order to make it possible for me to know you. Give me eyes to see past the temporal and into the eternal. Remind me to measure every supposed sacrifice by the standard you set at Calvary and by the certainty of eternity. You have shown the way. I pray for wisdom and courage to follow.

TOUCHSTONE

If you think the cost of discipleship is high, consider the price paid by those who refuse to be his disciples.

Therefore everyone who hears these words of mine and puts them into practice is like a wise man who built his house on the rock.   *Matthew 7:24*

Taking the Long Look

*I*n an address to the 1984 United States Olympic team, President Reagan made this comment: "You above all people know that it is not just the will to win that counts, but the will to prepare to win." Wherever there is the potential for great gain, there is usually the necessity for equal or greater sacrifice. Those who have excelled in their professions understand the relationship between accomplishment and sacrifice. Many believers are unaware of the fact that this same principle applies in the spiritual realm as well.

Jesus chose to communicate this important truth in a parable. Two men decided to build houses. One decided to take the easy way. He built his house on a river bank where the foundation would be easy to put in and materials were readily available. The other man chose the difficult task of hauling all his building supplies up to the top of a mountain. Once there, it took him days just to put in a foundation.

From the outset of the parable Jesus makes it clear who these two men represent. The first man represents that group of people who find the teachings of Christ too restrictive, too difficult to obey. The other builder represents those who are willing to pay the price of obedience. They are the few who are willing to put into "practice" what Jesus taught.

For a while it looked as if the man on the mountain had worked extra hard for nothing. But then the clouds began to gather. And soon the wind began to blow. Before long both houses were being battered by the wind. It was then that the man on the mountain began to fully enjoy the benefits of his hard labor. At the same time, his friend down below was probably thinking, "If only I had. . . ." But it was too late. And so it goes with those who cannot bring themselves to pay the price of obedience to Christ.

For many, freedom from sin involves pausing long enough to take the long look. What is it about Christ's teachings that you find too difficult to practice? No doubt you have the will to *endure* the storms of life. But willpower isn't enough. The real issue is, do you have the will *to prepare* for life's storms? Jesus was clear: obedience now ensures endurance later.

Heavenly Father, when obedience becomes difficult, remind me to take the long look. Bring to my mind the people in my life who are reaping the blessings of their decision to obey you when it wasn't convenient. Thank you for giving us principles that make for an enduring foundation. Use this truth to set me free from my spiritual nearsightedness. As I face life's storms, sustain me in such a way that others will be drawn to you. Amen.

TOUCHSTONE

Obedience to Christ enables us to endure the storms of life.

Take my yoke upon you and learn from me,
for I am gentle and humble in heart,
and you will find rest for your souls.   Matthew 11:29

The Yoke of Freedom

Generally speaking, we do not associate freedom with a yoke. The two concepts strike us as opposites. And yet the very one who said he came to set us free also invited us to share his yoke. Hmm. To complicate matters even further he promised *rest* for those who take him up on his offer. Once again we are confronted with what seems to be a contradiction in terms. How can one possibly find rest by putting on a yoke?

When Jesus spoke of a yoke, he was referring to a relationship—a relationship in which two would walk side by side in the same direction, covering the same ground, encountering the same obstacles, traveling at the same speed. By inviting his audience to submit to his yoke, he was asking them to come alongside him. In essence he was offering three things. First, he was offering to help shoulder their burden. Second, he was offering to guide them, for whenever two oxen were yoked together, one was always considered the lead animal. And third, Jesus was offering to instruct them in the ways of freedom.

The Savior knows how to keep your marriage free from the destructive forces prevalent in our society. He knows how to free your mind from jealousy, greed, and lust. He knows how to help you avoid becoming enslaved to destructive habits and attitudes. And so he invites you to come alongside him and learn the ways of freedom. He offers you an opportunity to walk beside him through the maze of attitudes, opportunities, and relationships that would threaten your liberty.

Many view the yoke of Christ as a threat to freedom. From their perspective a yoke is a yoke regardless of who it belongs to. It was for this very reason that Christ made his offer to the "weary and burdened" (Matt. 11:28)—those who had tried to find freedom on their own and had found only bondage instead. To those he said, "Come to me . . . and I will give you rest."

Has your quest for freedom led you to despair? Are you ready to come alongside the only One who can truly set you free?

Christ came that we might *experience* freedom, not just wish for it. Yet it is only when we humble ourselves and team up with him that personal freedom becomes a reality.

Heavenly Father, thank you for allowing me the privilege of intimacy with your Son. Thank you for the promise of rest and freedom. I willingly surrender myself to the teaching and instruction of the Lord Jesus. Give me ears to hear his voice and eyes to see his path. Lead me into freedom. Amen.

TOUCHSTONE

*By submitting ourselves to the
yoke of Christ today, we
ensure for ourselves the
freedom of Christ tomorrow.*

It is for freedom that Christ has set us free.
Stand firm, then, and do not let yourselves
be burdened again by a yoke of slavery.

Galatians 5:1

Standing Firm

*A*s Americans we have been blessed with a great deal of freedom. But our freedom was not without cost. Thousands of men and women sacrificed their lives to guarantee it. And thousands more are willing to do the same in order to maintain this valuable commodity. As long as there are forces in this world bent on stealing our freedom, there is the necessity of having men and women who focus on its preservation. So then, in the process of enjoying our freedom, we are constantly having to guard against those who would take it away.

The same principle holds true in the spiritual realm. Our independence from the domination of sin with all its trappings carried a high price tag. It cost God a great deal—his Son. Yet the battle for freedom did not end at Calvary. For it is only as we discover the truth and appropriate it that the liberty made available at the cross becomes a reality in our lives. But even then our struggle is not over. For there are forces all around us working to undermine our freedom. Whispers of condemnation, feelings of fear and insecurity, graceless messages from well-meaning pastors, constant criticism from those we love. Day after day our freedom is assailed from all sides.

It was this very threat that moved the apostle Paul to write, "Stand firm, then, and do not let yourselves be burdened again by a yoke of slavery." He knew from watching the Christians in Galatia that a believer's freedom must be constantly defended. For just as the truth can set us free, so the lies of the enemy can send us right back to the bondage we once knew.

Maintaining our spiritual freedom is much like defending our national freedom. In both cases we must guard against those who would rob us of our liberties. And in both cases the struggle is well worth the effort. What about you? Are you standing firm in the freedom Christ provided at the cross? Are you appropriating that truth daily? If not, take a few minutes to review the areas in which you know God wants to set you free. Today begin

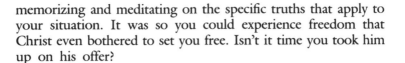

memorizing and meditating on the specific truths that apply to your situation. It was so you could experience freedom that Christ even bothered to set you free. Isn't it time you took him up on his offer?

Heavenly Father, thank you for sending Christ to pave the way for my freedom. Give me the wisdom to know how to protect this precious and costly gift. When I am bombarded by the lies intended to rob me of my Christian liberty, bring to my mind those truths that have proved themselves so effective against the weapons of our enemy. Use my freedom to draw others to yourself. And grant me the grace to continue standing firm. Amen.

TOUCHSTONE

Christ died to make us free; let us honor him by refusing to settle for anything less.

A Touch of His Wisdom

Contents

Photographs

Introduction

*W*hen I am faced with difficult decisions or challenges, I ask myself this question: "What is the wise thing to do?"

I am amazed at how often I turn to the book of Proverbs, where I discover so many of God's principles for wise living and decision making.

A Touch of His Wisdom is a collection of verses from each of the thirty-one chapters of Proverbs that have personally helped me to know and understand God's ways.

Wisdom is gaining God's perspective on life and applying it to particular circumstances. Proverbs clearly reveals his divine perspective on many of today's most pressing issues—morality, marriage, parenting, work, relationships, and finances, to name a few.

When I seek and apply God's wisdom, I can experience God's success rather than my failure. His order and peace replace my confusion, and I learn to lean on his faithfulness instead of succumbing to my fears or worries.

I am so glad that God is not reluctant to share his counsel with us. In fact, he says that if we lack wisdom, we can confidently ask for his insight and he will provide his timely answer (James 1:5–6).

It is my prayer that each of these chapters in *A Touch of His Wisdom* will reveal some facet of God's character and ways to help you in your daily Christian walk.

I pray along with the apostle Paul that God will "fill you with the knowledge of his will through all spiritual wisdom and understanding" (Col. 1:9).

The wise man or woman will bring honor to God through biblically sound decisions and will experience the priceless blessings of obedience to God.

Nothing can compare to knowing and obeying the wisdom of God. It is "more profitable than silver and yields better returns than gold" (Prov. 3:14).

A Touch of His Wisdom

The fear of the Lord is the beginning of knowledge.
Proverbs 1:7

The Foundation of Wisdom

*W*isdom is knowing and doing what is right. Not simply knowing, but making the right use of that knowledge. One may possess a vast storehouse of knowledge but still be unwise. True wisdom begins with a knowledge of and reverence for God as revealed through his Son Jesus Christ. This is the foundation on which to build a life that can courageously withstand the inevitable storms of criticism, pain, loss, temptation, and success.

The Scriptures are God's wisdom. They teach us who God is and reveal how he acts and thinks. They instruct us to distinguish right from wrong, and they give clear guidelines for practical living. His Word is counsel from heaven for life on earth, revealing the Father's omniscient heart to help us walk victoriously in all of our endeavors.

When learned and consistently applied, God's Word fastens firmly together the disjointed portions of our lives—our work, our family, our relationships, our dreams, our thoughts, our words, our deeds—in the sturdy framework of divine wisdom.

The starting point for distilling God's wisdom for everyday life is a profound reverence and honor for him. The "fear of the LORD" implies a sincere hatred and repentance of every sin (Prov. 8:13), combined with genuine, growing awe of his character, attributes, and personhood. (Ex. 15:11) One who fears God shuns evil and seeks good, cultivating his soul for the planting of God's Word.

We cannot know and honor God without first acknowledging our sin, receiving Christ's forgiveness, and establishing a new relationship with the Father through faith in Christ's work on the cross. Our knowledge grows as we depend on the power of the

Holy Spirit to impart to us the mind of Christ for every circumstance.

Each day can bring a new appreciation of the wonderful character and attributes of God—his holiness, righteousness, mercy, grace, love, and comfort. The more we worship, adore, and obey him, the more we experience the blessings of his wisdom.

A sincere reverence for God is the supernatural tool that embeds the Scriptures into the depths of our hearts, penetrating our innermost being with the ageless and perfect wisdom of the Carpenter from Nazareth.

The fear of the Lord is the foundation of a life built with wisdom. It is the first step toward a new adventure in knowing and following Jesus Christ.

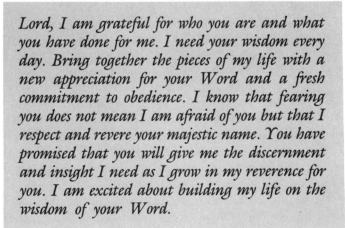

Lord, I am grateful for who you are and what you have done for me. I need your wisdom every day. Bring together the pieces of my life with a new appreciation for your Word and a fresh commitment to obedience. I know that fearing you does not mean I am afraid of you but that I respect and revere your majestic name. You have promised that you will give me the discernment and insight I need as I grow in my reverence for you. I am excited about building my life on the wisdom of your Word.

TOUCHSTONE

The life built on the wisdom of God endures forever.

Wisdom will enter your heart,
and knowledge will be pleasant to your soul.

Proverbs 2:10

Ask and Seek

God wants us to be wise. We, too, yearn for more wisdom and understanding. But how do we receive and grow in discernment and knowledge?

We recognize God as the source of all wisdom: "For the LORD gives wisdom, and from his mouth come knowledge and understanding" (Prov. 2:6).

If added together, all of the educational institutions in the world, all the books in all the libraries of every nation, and all the minds of the most astute intellectuals in every profession would be but a millimeter of intelligence compared to the fathomless mind of omniscient God—Creator, Sustainer, and End of all creation. Once we know him through faith in Christ, his flawless wisdom is accessible to counsel, guide, correct, and enlighten us in every circumstance, every problem, every need.

All we need to do to avail ourselves of his wisdom is ask. "If any of you lacks wisdom, he should ask God, who gives generously to all without finding fault, and it will be given to him" (James 1:5).

That almost seems too simple, doesn't it? We must remember, however, that we can know God and his ways only when he chooses to reveal himself and enlighten us through his Word and his Spirit. It is a matter of grace, and asking is the doorway to receiving the fullness of his grace.

Notice how abundantly and lavishly God gives. He does not begrudge us his wisdom according to our past behavior. He realizes our frailty and total dependence on him for fruitfulness, consistency, and maturity. His hand is overflowing with loving-kindness, extended without measure or limit.

When his father David died, Solomon became Israel's king. Although Solomon had the extraordinary education and amenities of a ruler's son, he knew he lacked the wisdom necessary to govern the nation of Israel.

One night the Lord appeared to Solomon in a dream and

made this astounding offer: "Ask for whatever you want me to give you" (1 Kings 3:5). Solomon's response was prompt: "Give your servant a discerning heart to govern your people and to distinguish between right and wrong" (v. 9).

Is that the cry of your heart? Would you rather gain riches, power, status, or beauty—or wisdom from God?

If you want wisdom, look to God only. Ask for it confidently. Eagerly anticipate his response. He is just as willing to impart his wisdom to you as he did to Solomon.

Wisdom should be our chief desire, and it *is* for the asking.

God, how desperately I need your wisdom and how grateful I am that you are the only wise God. Thank you that you liberally share your truth. I ask you for your wisdom and expect that I will have precisely the insight and information I need to do your will. Thank you for forgiving me my sins so that I can receive your wisdom by faith and grace. I have made many mistakes, but I hope to make far fewer as I learn more about you and apply your wisdom to my daily tasks.

TOUCHSTONE

Wisdom is for the asking.

Trust in the Lord with all your heart
and lean not on your own understanding;
in all your ways acknowledge him,
and he will make your paths straight.

Proverbs 3:5–6

Trust and Obey

W hen I was a teenager Proverbs 3:5–6 became my spiritual compass. Whenever I faced a difficult decision, I always turned to it for assurance. God etched its simple but profound truth in my mind and heart. It continues to be a signpost along life's road, ever pointing me to the bottom line for all decisions: trust and obey God. It is an eternal combination that always makes one a winner.

Why? Because God is trustworthy. He is dependable. He is sovereignly working everything together for his glory and our good.

His wisdom is given to those who look to him, lean on him, rely on him. The more we depend on our Father for instruction, strength, hope, and guidance, the more abundantly he confers on us his divine wisdom.

We cannot receive wisdom from God apart from a relationship with him. God is not interested in teaching his ways to those who have no desire to please him or follow him. He does yearn, however, to teach men and women who are bold enough to believe his promises and carry out his commands.

Trusting in the Lord means that we place our present and future circumstances in his hands, confident in his ability to orchestrate people and events to achieve his will. This whole-hearted trust brings a secure peace of mind and contentment. Putting our full emotional and volitional weight on the faithfulness of God activates his promises.

There is one catch, however. We must first admit our inadequacy: "Lean not on your own understanding." That was Solomon's attitude when he confessed, "But I am only a little child and do not know how to carry out my duties" (1 Kings 3:7).

This is where many Christians falter. We can do many things quite well without any apparent need for God's wisdom. We can repair items, invent machines, program computers, hike trails, and perform multitudes of other activities with very little sense of God's participation.

Yet we have been created by God to work in a world he fashioned with his own hands. Our lives, our very breath, is in his hands; our minds and bodies are his gifts. His wisdom is displayed in everything, even when we fail to recognize him.

God has given you talents and skills. However, they are maximized for eternity when you trust him to direct and use them for his plans. The question is, Will you lean on your own understanding or depend on God?

The wise choice is obvious when we understand that God knows the end from the beginning and sustains all things in between. Trusting him is the wisest decision we can make. Depending on our frail discernment limits us to a narrow, finite existence, restricted by circumstances and experiences we cannot control. Relying on God's wisdom adds a supernatural dimension that cannot be matched by anything on earth.

Father, keep me ever mindful of my inadequacy and your sufficiency. Continue to assure me that to lean on you is not a sign of weakness but of wisdom. I want always to remember that to obey you is not only right but always the wise choice—the decision that never fails to bring the richest rewards.

TOUCHSTONE

Trusting God is the wisest decision you can make.

Above all else, guard your heart,
for it is the wellspring of life.

Proverbs 4:23

The Wellspring
of Life

A small village heard about an enemy's plan to poison their
water supply. Although several small streams flowed
through the village, the leaders stationed their security force at
one location—the lone pool from where the springs flowed.
Their tactic worked perfectly. The security force seized the
saboteurs at dusk as they approached the pool.

Satan has a similar strategy. He launches his most damaging
assaults at the one area that most influences our behavior—the
heart. In the vocabulary of the Bible, the heart represents the
center of personality, soul, mind, will, and emotion.

The heart is the command and control system for our lives.
As God's wisdom is received and cultivated through the inner
working of the Holy Spirit, our lives reflect the presence and
influence of Jesus Christ. But to the extent that we neglect or
ignore the wellspring of the heart, our actions can become
polluted by our adversary, the Devil, damaging our relationships,
destroying our joy, and diluting our testimony.

We guard our hearts from sin's bitter defilement by
treasuring God's Word in our hearts (Ps. 119:9–11). The more
we study, meditate on, and practice the precepts of God, the safer
the inner sanctuary of our heart will be. God's Word cleanses us,
corrects us, exhorts us, encourages us, straining out impure
motivations and planting the seed of the Scriptures in our
innermost being.

We can also protect the wellspring of our soul by the
consistent exercise of prayer. Jesus instructed his disciples to
"watch and pray" so that they would not "fall into temptation"
(Matt. 26:41). Prayer is conscious fellowship with and dependence on Jesus Christ. When we pray with zeal and humility,
recognizing our frailty and God's power, we are alerted to the

Devil's deception and will turn quickly to the Father for his unfailing help.

Healthy, periodic self-examination is also a safeguard. Directed by the Holy Spirit, we ask God to search us and sift out any willful sin or camouflaged area of disobedience. "Watch your life and doctrine closely," Paul reminded Timothy (1 Tim. 4:16); and it is good advice for us as well. As the Spirit of God convicts us of sin or reveals an area of subtle rebellion, we repent and receive a fresh anointing and protection from God.

The issues of life, the essential matters, flow from the heart, determining the direction and impact of our lives. Guard your heart earnestly; and the wellspring of the Holy Spirit will overflow into all you do, say, and think.

Dear Father, I want you to establish your truth in my innermost being. I am sometimes so easily distracted and disturbed by outward circumstances that I neglect to cultivate a genuine devotion to you. Work through your Spirit to remove any false way and teach me to guard my heart through your indwelling presence. Control my thoughts and motivations and bring me into conformity with your will.

TOUCHSTONE

*Guard your heart, and you
will guard your life.*

For a man's ways are in full view of the Lord, and he examines all his paths.

Proverbs 5:21

Our God Who Really Sees

*W*hen Hagar was cast out of Abraham's camp because of Sarah's jealousy over her pregnancy, Hagar found herself abandoned on the roadside. There God met her with grace and love, promising her his help.

Grateful, she exclaimed, "You are the God who sees me" (Gen. 16:13). She ascribed a new name to God—El Roi, meaning "the God who really sees."

Our all-knowing, all-wise God is also our all-seeing God. His presence permeates all we do. We live and move and have our being in him. We walk before him each day, our hearts opened before him. He sees our pain, our discouragement, our confusion, our heartache, our struggles. And in the seeing, he comes to our rescue with amazing grace.

Understanding that every detail of our lives is laid bare before our heavenly Father and that we are in his all-sufficient care should move us to profound awe and adoration. We exclaim with David: "O LORD, you have searched me and you know me. You know when I sit and when I rise; you perceive my thoughts from afar. You discern my going out and my lying down; you are familiar with all my ways. Before a word is on my tongue you know it completely, O LORD. . . . Such knowledge is too wonderful for me, too lofty for me to attain" (Ps. 139:1–4, 6).

God sees your life from beginning to end. He numbered your days and ordered your steps while you were yet in your mother's womb. Seeing your plight brought about by sin, he sent his Son to save you from death and eternal destruction.

God's comprehensive knowledge of our ways should likewise encourage us to live obediently and honestly before him. It is futile for you to attempt to conceal your true feelings and actions. Even when you sin, you do so in the presence of God.

There is not one act, one thought, one ambition, one indiscretion that is hidden from his sight. "Nothing in all creation is hidden from God's sight. Everything is uncovered and laid bare before the eyes of him to whom we must give account" (Heb. 4:13).

Even our inner secrets are exposed to the penetrating gaze of God. Rather than frighten us, this should cause us to seek to please our Father, who treats us not according to our deeds but according to his mercy and grace in Jesus Christ.

We should be transparent in our relationship with him, realizing that even our foulest sins cannot separate us from his unfailing love. Our relationships with others should also be grounded on integrity and sincerity, as we attempt to avoid every form of hypocrisy.

The God who sees is the One who watches over us from before birth through death. He is with us and for us in all things, never condemning but always loving us.

Lord, I know that my entire life is an open book before you. How foolish I am to try to hide anything from you. I want to please you both privately and publicly, living in genuine honesty and hearty obedience. Thank you that you see my circumstances today and are at work in them to demonstrate your awesome power and mighty counsel.

TOUCHSTONE

Nothing can separate you from God's perfect love.

Can a man scoop fire into his lap
without his clothes being burned?
Can a man walk on hot coals
without his feet being scorched?

Proverbs 6:27–28

Truth or Consequences?

*W*isdom is the godly pathway to success, activating the blessings of God when we do his work in his way.

Decisions based on the faultless principles of the Scriptures will stand the test of time and criticism. Behavior motivated by loving obedience to God's commands will produce character that is solid and enduring, unaffected by the whims of circumstance and changing morality.

As surely as obedience to God's wisdom begets blessings, disobedience and rebellion ensure eventual chaos and disarray. When the Bible says the "wages of sin is death" (Rom. 6:23), it not only states sin's devastating penalty but also illustrates a divinely decreed principle: Sin always brings negative consequences.

We cannot act contrary to God's revealed truth and expect his favor and help. The apostle Paul put it this way: "Do not be deceived: God cannot be mocked. A man reaps what he sows" (Gal. 6:7).

Foolishness, the antithesis of biblical wisdom, will cause us to reap what we sow, more than we sow, later than we sow. Failure to comply with the truth of God's Word is thus a very serious and somber matter.

Each act of sin is a seed of insubordination to God's authority, planted in the soil of rebellion, bringing a bitter harvest. We cannot get away with sin. We cannot neglect the wisdom of God and expect to enjoy his blessings.

Even if we seemingly manage to avoid the consequences of disobedience, we will one day give an account of our actions before the Judge of all mankind. Justice will be righteously applied, resulting in the loss of reward for the believer and the loss of eternal relationship with God for the unbeliever.

God uses consequences to teach us the value of wisdom. We learn from the outcome of our mistakes that obeying God is far more pleasant and rewarding than neglecting or abusing his truth. Planting seeds of wisdom may be difficult at first, but the harvest is worth the effort.

The wise person lives in accord with God's Word because he knows the immeasurable riches of God's blessings. The foolish person's disobedience is compounded by the harsh and bitter consequences of his actions.

Do not get burned by the consequences of sin. Be wise and enjoy the blessings of submission to the Father's will.

Lord, I choose to be wise by obeying you. Nothing can compare to your blessings that come when I follow you. I know the danger of sin's consequences. Thank you for your grace to help me start anew each morning and for your Spirit to enable me to make the right choices.

TOUCHSTONE

*Before you sow, think of the
harvest you will reap.*

All at once he followed her
like an ox going to the slaughter,
like a deer stepping into a noose.

Proverbs 7:22

Run the Race

*W*hen soldiers go into battle, they must be very careful to tread only on ground that has been freed from land mines. A misplaced step into uncleared territory could be deadly.

Our cunning foe, the Devil, operates in similar fashion— concealing and camouflaging his real intentions by setting harmful snares of temptation and deceit. Human wisdom is no match in dealing with his cleverness and craftiness.

The best means to avoid his shrewd traps is to stay on the path of righteousness, walking straight forward in the will and ways of God.

The author of Hebrews termed this "the race marked out for us" (Heb. 12:1). The more we lean on Christ and the course he has marked out for us, the less likely we are to fall into Satan's traps.

But how do we keep on course? The author of Hebrews again provides the key: "Let us fix our eyes on Jesus, the author and perfecter of our faith" (Heb. 12:2).

Like a runner fixing his gaze on the finish line, the believer is to look away from all else that distracts from his personal relationship with Jesus Christ. There are many enticements along the way. Materialism. Success. Sensuality. The more attention we give to them, the more attractive their appeal becomes. To give in, however, is to give allegiance to someone or something other than the lordship of Christ.

The most effective defense is a steadfast gaze of the heart on the majesty and splendor of Jesus Christ. When we discover who he really is—and then dwell on his attributes of mercy, grace, love, holiness, and goodness and concentrate on his true nature—all else pales in comparison.

Keeping Jesus before us means spending daily time in his Word, maintaining a fresh and passionate prayer life, and consistently obeying the principles and truths we learn. Most important, it involves resolute faith in Christ and his promises.

The psalmist wrote about the person who loves the LORD: "His heart is steadfast, trusting in the Lord. His heart is secure, he will have no fear" (Ps. 112:7–8).

Jesus is faithful. He begins and completes your personal walk of faith as you rely on him. There is no temptation that he cannot overcome for you and with you. There is no evil that he cannot deliver you from. There is no obstacle that he cannot overcome on your behalf.

God never fails you. He will keep you from the Evil One by keeping you on the path of righteousness—for his name's sake, by his own power, for his own glory.

Just look to him.

I realize, Lord, that I cannot detect or avoid Satan's subtle snares in my own strength. I need you to help me "run the race" you have charted for my life. Equip me and guide me so that I may not be detoured or distracted from your will. Thank you for making me stand upright again after I do fall.

TOUCHSTONE

*Keep your eyes on Jesus and
off your circumstances.*

Choose my instruction instead of silver,
knowledge rather than choice gold.

Proverbs 8:10

Going Against the Flow

God's wisdom must be deliberately chosen. We never drift into wisdom. We must make a conscious decision to seek and receive God's divine counsel and instruction: "We must pay more careful attention, therefore, to what we have heard, so that we do not drift away" (Heb. 2:1).

The Mississippi River flows several hundred miles through the heartland of America, surging to its end in southern Louisiana, spilling its last breath into the Gulf of Mexico. For almost its entire length, its banks are littered with debris and driftwood that became caught up in its enormous torrent and were tossed aside along its meandering journey.

Unless we make a definite choice to pursue wisdom, we, too, can become swept up in the appealing currents of our age. There are swift tides of human pleasure and attraction that can captivate any believer who is not fully committed to Jesus as Savior, Lord, and Life.

His ways and thoughts are not ours (Isa. 55:8). We should think and act contrary to the world's stream of thought. God says you give to receive; the world says hoard all you can. God says you succeed by serving; the world defines success as upward mobility. God says you are to love your enemies; the world tells you to seek revenge.

Choosing God's wisdom begins with realizing its value: "For wisdom is more precious than rubies, and nothing you desire can compare with her" (Prov. 8:11). The wisdom of God is priceless, without peer. Its worth cannot be calculated. All the riches of the universe are like a beggar's hand when compared to the worth of God's wisdom.

Once we perceive the value of God's wisdom, we realize its unlimited application. It touches all of life, imparting his

supernatural perspective to all we do and say. His wisdom works anywhere, anytime, in any situation. Its yield of peace, commitment, joy, and blessing is far superior to money, possessions, or status.

Our task is to listen and obey: "Blessed is the man who listens to me, watching daily at my doors, waiting at my doorway" (Prov. 8:34).

Choose God's wisdom. Refuse to be ensnared by the world's deceptions. Dare to trust in the instruction of Christ, diligently cultivating and earnestly appropriating the counsel of God.

Pay close attention to what the Father says. Esteem him above all else, and your life will bear the unmistakable and inestimable fruit of godly wisdom.

Living against the world's flow is difficult, Lord. I want your wisdom, but sometimes I seem to be caught up in so many of this culture's currents. I choose today to seek and pursue your ways. I make this decision in prayerful dependence on you to impart your wisdom to me and teach me your ways. I choose to listen to you daily so I may enjoy the benefits of godly wisdom.

TOUCHSTONE

We never drift into wisdom.

Instruct a wise man and he will be wiser still;
teach a righteous man and he will add to his learning.

Proverbs 9:9

The Classroom of Wisdom

*S*chool is never out for true saints. They long with unceasing fervor to learn of and know Christ more intimately—the Christ in whom are hidden all the treasures of wisdom and knowledge.

Wisdom cannot be reduced to a formula. It is a right relationship with Christ that provides a biblical context so that we can make wise decisions for every phase of living. However, there is a sacred principle that constitutes an eternal equation for receiving and applying God's wisdom: The degree of wisdom we possess from God is directly proportional to our spirit of humility.

A wise person is not a proud one. Pride and vanity are like poison to the spirit of wisdom. Whoever thinks he is wise is disqualified from God's classroom, where wisdom is given to the contrite of spirit and humble of heart.

Christianity is a growing experience, a deepening relationship with the Savior. You are always in a learning mode as a disciple—literally, a learner—of Jesus Christ. The apostle Paul exemplified the spirit of wisdom when he said, "Not that I have already obtained all this, or have already been made perfect, but I press on to take hold of that for which Christ Jesus took hold of me" (Phil. 3:12).

As believers we must never spend time on the plateau of past accomplishments or present achievements. We must realize we can never plumb the depths of God's wisdom, never exhaust his boundless supply. We should constantly press on to know God (Hos. 6:3), always learning, always seated at the feet of the Master, always awed by the glory and grace of God.

The wise learner understands he is totally dependent on God to reveal his truth. One cannot come to know and fellowship intimately with Christ apart from the benevolent ministry of the Holy Spirit who guides, corrects, instructs, and exhorts. The wise learner is careful to give credit to God alone and not to "venture to speak of anything except what Christ has accomplished through [him]" (Rom. 15:18).

The disciple of Christ learns and matures through Christ's discipline and chastisement. He does not pout or sulk when reproved but understands that the path of godly wisdom is his complete acceptance of God's correction and forgiveness for all his mistakes. Failures are not dead ends but valuable lessons to distill truth from error.

Are you a learner? Do you hunger and thirst for righteousness? Or have you settled for a mediocre life, satisfied with a nominal knowledge of Christ? Wisdom is imparted to the eager student, the meek spirit, the probing mind, the open heart, the repentant soul. Such a person prays, "Show me your ways, O LORD, teach me your paths" (Ps. 25:4).

Are you willing to come to Christ and learn of him?

Father, I realize I am a student in your divine classroom. Place within my heart a thirst to know you and your ways. Then I shall be wise.

TOUCHSTONE

Don't be a dropout in the school of wisdom.

When words are many, sin is not absent,
but he who holds his tongue is wise.

Proverbs 10:19

Tongue Twisters

During the Second World War, the government of Great Britain was concerned about the infiltration of enemy spies and the security risks they posed. To minimize the danger, government officials placed large posters throughout the nation with this admonition: *Careless talk costs lives.*

Proper use of the tongue is the fruit of wisdom. Careless talk—gossip, innuendo, slander, criticism—hurts people, severs personal relationships, generates hostility and bitterness, and creates discord that can influence generations.

James referred to the tongue as an instrument that charts the course of our lives, making our way smooth or rough, depending on its use. It is a spiritual and emotional rudder, steering us either into conflict or into blessing (James 3:3–8).

When it is used as an instrument of righteousness, in keeping with God's intentions, the tongue is a "fountain of life" (Prov. 10:11), refreshing the discouraged soul. It is as "choice silver" (v. 20), a priceless possession for peaceful, contented living. "The lips of the righteous nourish many" (v. 21), instructing others with the solid truth of God's Word. "The mouth of the righteous brings forth wisdom" (v. 31), giving practical, sound counsel and knows "what is fitting" (v. 32), giving the right answer at the right time.

The wise man's tongue heals, teaches, blesses, encourages, comforts, and promotes godliness. Isn't that what we all desire but find so difficult to achieve?

Speaking words of wisdom begins with a profound transformation of thinking. A person speaks from the treasure of his heart. Our words are but the public pronouncement of the private place of the heart. David said, "May the words of my mouth and the meditation of my heart be pleasing in your sight, O Lord, my Rock and my Redeemer" (Ps. 19:14).

Ask the Holy Spirit to produce in you the fruit of godly speech by working the soil of your heart with his kindness and

goodness. Esteem others more important than yourself and realize that when you speak disparagingly of another, you are belittling God's special and beloved creation.

Resolve not to speak evil of a person who is not in your presence. Most unruly speech is found in discussions about a third person where only two are gathered. Allow God to tame your speech by quieting the tongue. "When words are many, sin is not absent, but he who holds his tongue is wise" (Prov. 10:19). Refrain from the urge to always express your opinion.

God can use your speech to praise him and edify others, leaving behind a harvest of righteousness that bears fruit in the lives of many people. Allow God to guard your lips by sifting what flows into your mind and filtering what flows out through the purity of his Holy Spirit. You will be amazed at the difference a wise tongue can make.

I must admit, Lord, I have great trouble controlling my tongue. In fact, I can't. Unless you work in my heart to transform my thinking, my words will reveal the ugliness of sin. Cleanse me from my unrighteousness. Show me how to reduce my volume of words while you cleanse me and implant your wisdom in my heart. I want to bless others with my tongue, not hurt them. Make my mouth an instrument of righteousness through the power of the Holy Spirit, who resides at the fountainhead of my speech—my heart.

TOUCHSTONE

Control your tongue, or your tongue will control you.

*A generous man will prosper;
and he who refreshes others
will himself be refreshed.*

Proverbs 11:25

Give, and
It Won't Hurt

*T*he apostle Paul said that the sum of wisdom, the height and depth and breadth of its infinite storehouse, is found in Christ "in whom are hidden all the treasures of wisdom and knowledge" (Col. 2:3).

However, Jesus does not hoard his wisdom. Rather, he gives without measure. He gives his grace abundantly. He gives his guidance freely. He gives his comfort lovingly. The ultimate expression of giving came on the cross where he willingly sacrificed himself for man: "He who did not spare his own Son, but gave him up for us all—how will he not also, along with him, graciously give us all things?" (Rom. 8:32).

It is the very nature of God to give. All good things come from above, from his open hand and benevolent heart. Made in his image, we, too, are called to be generous people, extending the goodness of God to others.

We can adopt a lifestyle of giving because God has first given to us. His divine resources are available to us through our relationship with Christ and the presence of the Holy Spirit.

Our first step toward becoming generous people is giving to God. It is our means of acknowledging his lordship and demonstrating our dependence on him. A good beginning is to give a tithe, a tenth of what we earn. This becomes easier when we understand that everything rightfully belongs to God. Returning a fraction of his liberality should delight us. We are to give gleefully, gratefully, humbly.

Obedience in this area enables us to bless others as God honors our commitment. Giving ignites an explosion of divine grace and abundance: "And God is able to make all grace abound to you, so that in all things at all times, having all that you need, you will abound in every good work" (2 Cor. 9:8).

The pump primed by honoring God, pouring forth a torrent of God's spiritual riches, is at our disposal to help others. We can share encouraging words to the discouraged, for we are encouraged by him. We can serve the needs of the emotionally and spiritually impoverished, for he also took on the form of a servant. We can give our friendship to the lonely, for he is our unfailing Friend.

Each act of giving, whatever form it may take, is a divine seed that multiplies our joy and peace. There has never been a time when God did not honor a giving heart. It is a spiritual law for contented, fruitful living in the kingdom of God.

All that we have—salvation, eternal and physical life, and daily sustenance—comes from the Father above. He made you and me so that we could receive his choicest treasure, our relationship with him for eternity.

Our cheerful response should be to imitate him. Give of yourself and your possessions to him and others. Your spirit of generosity will be a fountain of supernatural refreshment to thirsty and needy men and women.

"Give, and it will be given to you" (Luke 6:38).

I can hardly understand your love, heavenly Father. You gave your only Son for my sins, and you continue to give me all that I need each day. Teach me to give of myself to others so that your storehouse of spiritual riches may overflow through me. Do not let me be selfish. Free me from greed so that I may participate in your grand scheme of grace and giving.

TOUCHSTONE

You can never outgive God.

*Whoever loves discipline loves knowledge,
but he who hates correction is stupid.*

Proverbs 12:1

Don't Be Stupid

*T*he Bible uses the word *stupid* on rare occasions. When it does, we should take heed.

The foolish man in the Scriptures is the one who fails to receive correction. He spurns and ignores it, refusing its counsel. Pride, ego, and plain stubbornness are often the limp excuses for rejecting the reproofs of wisdom.

However, the correction that God gives is actually a remarkable sign of his great love for us. Jesus said, "Those whom I love I rebuke and discipline" (Rev. 3:19).

Like a concerned parent, God corrects his children who are on a wayward path: "The Lord disciplines those he loves, and he punishes everyone he accepts as a son" (Heb. 12:6).

Does that change your view of admonition? Do you see that God's sometimes painful dealings with you are but an extension of his fatherhood? Do you understand that his rebuke only affirms your glorious position as a child of God, who loves you enough to place his disciplining hand on your life?

When you were a child, your mother or father corrected you frequently. Unfortunately, not all of their reprimands were from pure motivations. They probably were angry, upset, or even unjust at times.

This is not the case with the discipline of our heavenly Father. His reproofs are always loving, just, and perfect. He never rebukes us in anger, never seeks to harm us or belittle us. His correction is for our welfare, for our success, for our enlightenment. Because he knows all things, he knows that our unwise actions or thoughts will lead to our eventual destruction; and in his mercy and grace, he intervenes with his kind but firm reproof.

His usual agent of correction is his living Word: "All Scripture is God-breathed and is useful for teaching, rebuking, correcting and training in righteousness" (2 Tim. 3:16). The

Scriptures encourage and guide us, but they frequently do so by pointing out our misconceptions, blunders, and deficiencies.

Our response should be one of immense thanksgiving that through the ministry of his Word God is able to correct our erroneous course. Rather than becoming discouraged, hurt, or combative when God examines us, we should be quick to examine ourselves, repent, and allow the Holy Spirit to direct our steps in his straight path.

God loves you dearly. He is willing to discipline you in order that you may share in his holiness and enjoy the blessings he has in store for the obedient Christian. Don't be "stupid." The rod of God keeps you in his safe pasture and protects you from the consequences of foolish decisions.

I have to confess, Father, that I don't like discipline. Give me discernment to know when you are correcting me. Help me not to pout or become angry, but accept your correction as a demonstration of your love for me.

TOUCHSTONE

*God's correction always steers
us into his love.*

He who walks with the wise grows wise,
but a companion of fools suffers harm.
> **Proverbs 13:20**

The Friendship Factor

*M*y grandfather had a profound influence on my life and ministry. The occasion I had to sit and talk with him about his walk with God not only became a cornerstone in my understanding and relationship with Christ; it also set the direction for my ministry, and I have never wavered from it. It was not what he told me about God that made such an inescapable impression, but what he experienced with God.

Getting to know godly men and women is a choice tool for cultivating the wisdom of God. People who hunger and thirst for God and whose lives exemplify the fruit of the Holy Spirit have much to teach us about the principles of the Scriptures and the character of God. They do not merely possess information about God; they have tested and proved his faithfulness through the years.

If you would like to grow in wisdom, first pray for God to lead you to the persons of his choice to become your close friends. We sometimes think we know best when it comes to establishing Christian friendships. But only God knows the heart, and only God knows who is best equipped to minister to our specific needs and hurts. He knows who can bring God's comfort to us, who can deepen our perspective about his ways, and whose personal experiences can bring his helpful instruction and guidance to our circumstances.

Spiritual maturity is a key. Wisdom is not learned in the course of months or even years. It resides in the one who has endured, who has suffered, who has been sustained by God in times of doubt, adversity, and opposition. This does not mean that spiritual maturity and age always go hand in hand, but it does mean that the individuals you befriend should have some spiritual mileage under their belts.

Look for an encourager. God wants to bless you, to edify you. That may involve correction; but his correction is always given in love and truth, not condemnation. We need to be built

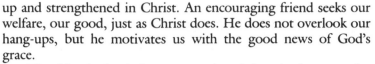

up and strengthened in Christ. An encouraging friend seeks our welfare, our good, just as Christ does. He does not overlook our hang-ups, but he motivates us with the good news of God's grace.

The friend who helps us grow in wisdom is also one who hungers and thirsts for God. He is a learner. He is not conceited or prideful and is not afraid to admit his own failures, for we learn from mistakes as well as successes.

Once God directs us to those individuals he has chosen, we need to persevere in our relationships with them. Seek opportunities to spend time with them. There will be all kinds of distractions, but we must "walk with the wise" if we are to become wise.

God-ordained friendships are sharp tools for producing Christlikeness in our lives. You cannot think of David apart from Jonathan; Elisha without Elijah; or Paul without Timothy, Barnabas, or Silas.

Are you learning about God from a wise Christian? It is an adventure that will transform you and prepare you to bring God's truth to others who also need to trust and know him.

Lord, direct me to a friend who will enable me to know you better, one whose walk will inspire me, reprove me, and build me into Christlikeness. Thank you for the people you have already placed in my life and the ones you will direct me to in the future.

TOUCHSTONE

*Godly friends help you draw
near to God.*

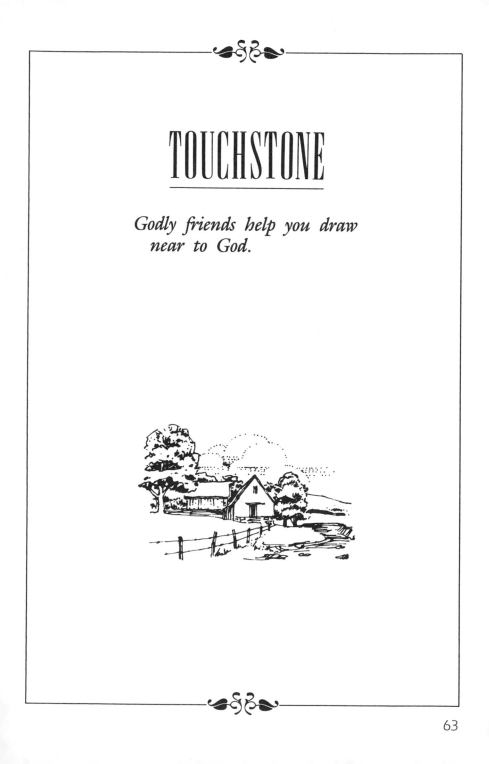

A simple man believes anything,
but a prudent man gives thought to his steps.
Proverbs 14:15

Think About It

*O*n many occasions before making important decisions, I ask the Lord this question: "What is the wise thing to do?" While God is ultimately in charge of providing the answer, every believer is responsible for exercising what the Scriptures call "prudence."

Prudence is often used as a synonym for *wisdom*. The prudent man or woman is responsible for using spiritual discernment in practical affairs. The prudent person can avoid unnecessary frustration, failure, and disappointment and can reap the blessings of godly wisdom.

Prudence begins with the gathering of pertinent information. When Moses sent twelve spies into Canaan, he wanted some facts. "What kind of land do they live in? Is it good or bad? What kind of towns do they live in? Are they unwalled or fortified? How is the soil? Is it fertile or poor? Are there trees on it or not?" (Num. 13:19–20). Although God had promised Moses that he would bring the people of Israel into Canaan, Moses was still responsible for appraising the situation wisely.

The purpose for collecting facts is to examine them thoroughly and investigate the information from a godly perspective. We are to sift the facts through the supernatural grid of prayer and God's Word. As we pray about the matter, using the Scriptures as our guide, God works to show us his will and direction. The twelve men brought back an accurate report of the condition of the land and people of Canaan, but ten of them failed to align the facts with God's promise of deliverance.

Like Joshua and Caleb, we must bring the facts before the revealed truth of God's Word. The Word of God sheds supernatural light on our decision-making process. Joshua and Caleb were prudent because they faithfully exercised their task of gathering and analyzing information *and* trusted God for the results.

The prudent person understands that only God knows the

future. We cannot always know all the facts. We cannot forecast the future. However, we can entrust each decision into the sovereign hand of God. Joshua and Caleb knew the promise of God to deliver them from the giant residents of Canaan, but they had to trust him to fulfill his pledge.

Prudence is doing all we can to make responsible, wise decisions while placing our complete faith in God's providence and faithfulness. When we do so, we can count on God's encouraging and faith-building direction.

Father, I don't often look before I leap. My landings are not pretty. Help me to take the time to look things over thoroughly when making important decisions. Let me know what you want, and I will trust you for the outcome.

TOUCHSTONE

Always ask, "What is the wise thing to do?"

The Lord is far from the wicked
but he hears the prayer of the righteous.

Proverbs 15:29

Is Anybody Listening?

*D*oes God hear your prayers?

David wrote that if he "had cherished sin in [his] heart, the Lord would not have listened" (Ps. 66:18). James said that our prayers can be powerful and effective, but they must come from a "righteous" person (James 5:16).

Doesn't that count us out? Don't we all secretly harbor sin of one sort or another in our souls? And if the competence of our prayer life is based on the degree of our righteousness, do we not all fall short?

If our response to these questions is based on our own feelings or spiritual effort, we would have to conclude that God seldom hears our prayers and that the prayers that do reach the Father are weak. However, when we understand the radical good news of the Gospel, we can joyfully declare that God hears our every word, is intimately acquainted with every thought, and is eager to respond to the slightest utterance of our heart or lips.

Here's why. The cross of Christ, the pivotal point and cornerstone of eternity, provided the divine answer to both of these dilemmas. At Calvary, our sin was forgiven, not just our past sins before we were saved but all of our sins—past, present, and future. We are a forgiven people. There is no need for false guilt or condemnation. Confession is still essential to keeping your relationship with Christ intimate, but your sins can never keep you from enjoying your eternal position as a forgiven child of God. Your sin account with God is cleared, settled by the death of Christ. Your sins, all of them, have been carried away by Christ. If the Holy Spirit convicts you of a specific sin, agree that it is an offense to God, repent, and move on.

Better yet, in the cross of Christ God not only forgave you all your sins, but he also attributed the righteousness of Christ to you. Sin was taken away, and the righteousness of God was credited to you. You do not work to attain that righteousness,

you simply received it by faith when you accepted Jesus as your Savior.

Righteousness is a condition of unending acceptability by God. You will never be more righteous than you are right now. At the core of your identity in Christ you are completely righteous, holy, and blameless. You can never become unrighteous or rejected because of your behavior. You may be disciplined or chastened by God if you sin, but God will never change your status as his righteous child.

The prayers of a righteous person are heard; and that is what you are, the righteousness of God in Christ Jesus (2 Cor. 5:21). Pray fervently. Pray always. God's ear is continually open to the cry of the righteous, and your sins are cast into the depths of the sea.

Thank you, Lord, that my performance does not turn you away from me. I am so glad you have made me righteous for all eternity and that you are always tuned to my heart's cry.

TOUCHSTONE

You are as righteous in Christ today as you ever will be.

Whoever gives heed to instruction prospers,
and blessed is he who trusts in the Lord.

Proverbs 16:20

Leaning on Jesus

I observed a man repairing lines on a telephone pole outside my home one day. Despite the height, he worked with apparent ease and dispatch, securely leaning his entire weight on a thick leather safety belt.

That is what trusting the Lord is like. We go about our appointed rounds at work and at home, tackling an assortment of tasks. On the surface, it may appear that we work in our own sufficiency; but we realize that our spiritual success depends on leaning our emotional, spiritual, and volitional weight on the Lord Jesus Christ. He is the source of our strength and security. We are dependent on him. Our times are in his hands.

Trusting in the Lord, leaning on his adequacy, is possible as we anchor our confidence in the promises of God. There are some fearful moments in life, times when we doubt, times of confusion and anxiety. Then, when circumstances are less than favorable, nothing is more comforting or stabilizing than looking to the Scriptures for support and direction. God's Word is sure. It never fails—not one word. It ministers to our deepest needs and speaks to our innermost being. When we place our faith in God's Word, we accept it as his truth, despite our wavering feelings. We simply believe that God means what he says and that he will fulfill all his promises.

We also lean our weight on Christ by affirming the character of God. We can trust in his Word because he is trustworthy. We can count on his help because he is faithful. The attributes of God—such as his holiness, goodness, mercy, justice, and grace—anchor our faith in him. The better we know him, the more we trust him. The more we trust him, the more we see his hand at work in our midst.

Perhaps one of the most significant ways that we place our full trust in Christ is by praising him regardless of the circumstances. Praise shouts our faith in God. It exalts him and declares that we will follow him and look to him even when the

odds appear against us. As we praise God, we magnify the majesty and greatness of our Father. We focus on who God is, and that is a divinely given catalyst for trusting him still more. Praise drives away fear and builds faith.

The person who trusts in the Lord is blessed. He clings to the promises of God, delights in the character of God, and worships God in darkness or in light. He leans on the everlasting arms that never fail or forsake him.

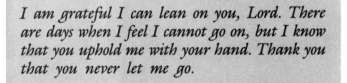

I am grateful I can lean on you, Lord. There are days when I feel I cannot go on, but I know that you uphold me with your hand. Thank you that you never let me go.

TOUCHSTONE

When you lean on Jesus, your footing is always firm.

He who covers over an offense promotes love.
Proverbs 17:9

An Upward Promotion

*M*any believers are good record-keepers. They tend to tally the offenses of others against them, keeping an up-to-date emotional track record of their hurts. The unfortunate sum of such tabulations is strife, anger, bitterness, and resentment.

The way of wisdom in dealing with those who wrong us is the way of love. Jesus' work of reconciliation on the cross destroyed any record of our sins against God. "God was reconciling the world to himself in Christ, not counting men's sins against them" (2 Cor. 5:19). God no longer keeps any summary sheet of our wrongs. He has chosen instead to forgive us when we, by faith, receive the gift of his Son, Jesus Christ.

Who are we, then, to harbor grudges against those who wound us? If Jesus, whom all sin is ultimately against, has covered our sins with his cleansing love, how can we fail to extend his love to others?

How does God love us? Unconditionally. Without strings. Without limit. How are we to love others? The same way, according to the apostle Paul. Christian love "keeps no record of wrongs" (1 Cor. 13:5). When you choose to forgive another his offense against you, you erase the mental tally sheet of his trespass. It is possible that you may not forget—but, like God, you choose not to hold the offender in emotional debt to you.

How do you extend such love? When we experience the extraordinary, forgiving love of God because Christ died for us, we express the healing power of that love by dying to self. We choose to die to our rights. We deliberately decide in obedience to Christ and his Word to forfeit any right of retaliation or revenge. Only then is the love of God able to be released by the power of the Holy Spirit. Is it difficult? It certainly is. Does it happen without a struggle? Almost never. But it does enable us to forgive others as Christ has forgiven us.

Promoting love does not come naturally to us, but it is the very nature of our God, who is Love and who is our Life. Each time we release his love through an act of forgiveness, we extend the same grace he has given to us and continues to give. "Do not repay evil with evil or insult with insult, but with blessing, because to this you were called so you may inherit a blessing" (1 Peter 3:9). Be a blessing and inherit the peace, joy, and righteousness of the kingdom of God by promoting his love to those who hurt you.

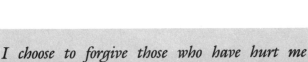

I choose to forgive those who have hurt me because you tell me that is what I am to do, Lord. How can I withhold your love from others when you so freely love me? Let me always take the initiative to extend your love to others.

TOUCHSTONE

Each time you forgive, you choose freedom in Christ.

He who answers before listening—
that is his folly and his shame.

Proverbs 18:13

God Is Still Speaking

*F*or forty-seven years I have been a follower of Christ. One of the most practical, exciting, and rewarding lessons has been learning to listen to God. It is the key to knowing him and walking in his will. It is absolutely essential to an intimate relationship with Christ, which should be the goal of every believer.

Cultivating the essential art of listening is a vital discipline for developing godly wisdom. Practical James wrote that "everyone should be quick to listen, slow to speak and slow to become angry" (James 1:19). His admonition obviously cuts across our natural grain of freely expressing our own opinions, whether we are asked for them or not, and underscores God's desire to heighten our receptivity to himself and others.

Listening to God is crucial for a mature Christian walk. God is still speaking today because he wants to communicate his will and love to us just as much as he did to the people of Bible times. We hear his voice primarily through his Word. The Holy Spirit impresses a verse or providentially arranges circumstances so that we may hear, see, and experience the wonder of his guidance and provision.

God also speaks to us through the wisdom of other people. He is at work in all of his obedient children who bring God's Word of encouragement or enlightenment at just the right moment. How important, then, that we learn to let others share with us, to adopt the position of a hearer. The Scriptures tell us we are to consider others better than ourselves (Phil. 2:3). That doesn't mean only those Christians who are impressive, but all believers. God can use the most lowly of his children, even a child, to communicate his will.

However, hearing God speak is difficult to the one intent on merely making his own petitions known. We must be quiet in our spirit, at rest in our souls, asking God to speak clearly to us through his Word. Nothing compares to the thrill of knowing

that God has spoken directly to our particular circumstances. His speaking through his Word in this way is an expression of his love and care in every detail of our lives.

Listening carefully to God and other Christians allows us to have the full input of supernatural revelation before making decisions. It places us in the humble posture of a learner who desires above all to hear the voice of God. God is still speaking. Are you listening?

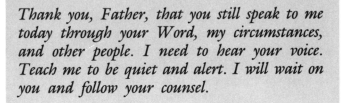

Thank you, Father, that you still speak to me today through your Word, my circumstances, and other people. I need to hear your voice. Teach me to be quiet and alert. I will wait on you and follow your counsel.

TOUCHSTONE

Listening to God is the way of wisdom.

A man's wisdom gives him patience.

Proverbs 19:11

Perfect Timing

R ight timing is critical. It is crucial for success in warfare, in science, in sports, in business deals, in relationships, and in just about any other endeavor of everyday living. But did you know that right timing is equally significant in your spiritual walk? And did you know that God requires your timely cooperation with him to fulfill his plan for you?

Almost invariably, discovering and cooperating with God's perfect timing requires waiting on him. We are impatient creatures. We become easily frustrated, irritated, and often discouraged when we encounter obstacles that delay or hinder us. But God is always on time, never late. He is never thwarted by any circumstance; and when we choose to wait for his timing, we position ourselves for God's maximum blessing.

Waiting on God is not an irksome, boring task. It is one of the most exciting activities a believer can participate in because the rewards are so incredible. It is not a passive attitude but a dynamic expectation, as we focus our attention through persistent prayer and meditation on God's Word. It is a deliberate setting of the mind, heart, and will to know and do the will of the Father at all costs. It is a matter of rejecting our fear of failure, refusing to yield to the unwise opinions of others, and steadfastly resisting the urge to move recklessly ahead when we are unsure of God's plan.

When we foolishly launch out on our timetable instead of God's, we miss God's best for our lives. The prophet Samuel told King Saul to wait for him at Gilgal for seven days. When Samuel did not show, Saul felt compelled to offer the burnt offering himself and thus forfeited his kingship over Israel. Consequently, God decided to find a man after his own heart (1 Sam. 13:12–14). That man was David, who, more than any other author of Scripture, wrote about waiting on God. David acknowledged God's plan and timing for his life by refusing to take advantage of two opportunities to slay Saul. After Saul was killed by his own sword, David became the king of Judah. However, he waited on God for seven more years before the men of Israel asked him to reign over them as well. When he became their king, David could confidently say that he "knew that the LORD had established him as king over Israel" (2 Sam. 5:12).

When we wait for God's perfect timing, we *know* that God has directed us and blessed us. We taste of his goodness and grace. We have the sheer joy of experiencing God's magnificent care and provision. We see his answer to prayer. We discover his good and perfect will. We know God is working on our behalf. We win the battles of life by waiting steadfastly on God, who accomplishes all things on our behalf. Wait patiently on him in every circumstance, and you will be a person after God's own heart. There is no higher blessing.

I am quick to get ahead of you, Father. I am so impatient. Teach me to wait on you without being passive. I have many things to do, but nothing is more important than waiting for your timing.

TOUCHSTONE

God is never late.

A man's steps are directed by the Lord.
How then can anyone understand his own way?
Proverbs 20:24

Under Construction

I watched some interstate road construction with great interest recently. A small overpass that had been built in the beginning phases of construction appeared hopelessly disconnected to the entire project. There were no roads leading to or from the overpass; it was just a span of concrete that seemed to lead nowhere. However, when the project was completed, the seemingly misplaced overpass proved to be a vital link at a heavily traveled interstate junction.

Sometimes our lives can seem a bit like that. We are not sure why we are working at that particular job, living in this particular city, or attending this particular school. We simply do not see how it fits into God's scheme of things.

It is exactly at this juncture that we must rely on the sovereignty of God. God knows what he desires to accomplish in our lives. He is aware of how this day, this job, this relationship is pieced together in his good and acceptable plan. You see, our wisdom has limits. We do not know what a day will bring forth. However, God's wisdom is infinite and transcendent. He weaves every thread of our existence into a purposeful, productive, profitable plan.

When I decided many years ago to come to First Baptist Church of Atlanta, I was pastoring a growing, thriving church, and I was perfectly content there. I was not sure why I should move, but I knew God was directing me to do so.

The first few years in Atlanta were intensely stressful. However, we steadily grew, and God opened a small door for the *In Touch* broadcast. Today these broadcasts can be heard worldwide.

More than twenty years ago, I could never have foreseen either the struggles or the successes of this ministry. I simply obeyed God and trusted him. And that is the key to bringing order and meaning to what seems like chaotic, meaningless seasons in our lives. Somehow Joseph understood that principle several thousand years ago. At age seventeen he enjoyed the prosperity of a prominent Hebrew family. For the next thirteen years, he worked as a servant in a foreign land and spent time in an Egyptian jail. In each experience, though, Joseph's steady hand and diligence caused him to find favor with God. He did the best with what he had, did what he knew to be right, and trusted God. He did not know at seventeen years of age that he would administer the Egyptian kingdom at thirty.

God uses *everything* for good in your life when you entrust yourself and your circumstances to his providential control. No situation is hopeless. No problem is outside his love, wisdom, or sovereignty. You may not understand the present state of your life, but God does. Rest in his sufficiency and sovereignty.

I must confess, Lord, that there are seasons in my life that seem futile. When I don't understand, it is comforting and reassuring to know that you have a purpose for everything in my life. Thank you for your sovereignty.

TOUCHSTONE

God is in control.

The king's heart is in the hand of the Lord;
he directs it like a watercourse wherever he pleases.
Proverbs 21:1

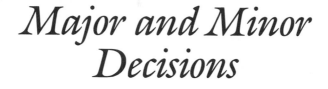

Major and Minor Decisions

*W*hen facing major or minor decisions in life, I always ask, "What would obedience to God require of me?" My choice must never be based on the possible outcome of my decision, but rather on what God would have me do. That requires me to place my own will in neutral so that God can move me in his direction. It also requires me to be cautious in listening to the many voices of counsel that may be contrary to his guidance. Like everyone else, I am prone to give undue emphasis to particular pieces of information or words of counsel.

Our "heart is in the hand of the Lord" when we are fully surrendered to Jesus Christ as Lord. Jesus is our Savior, Lord, and Life. He asks for total submission of our total being to him. Surrender has negative connotations in our society. It is usually coupled with defeat and weakness. However, in the spiritual realm, surrender is always linked to victory and success. It is the means by which we confess that God knows what is best for us as we yield our rights to him. It is the acceptance of his lordship. When I tell Jesus that I truly want his wisdom and his will, I become clay in the Potter's hand, a sheep of his pasture, dependent on him for guidance and protection.

The surrendered heart is also a sifted heart. I allow God to sift my motivations. Do I really want to honor and glorify Christ in this matter, or am I seeking to exalt myself? "All a man's ways seem right to him, but the LORD weighs the heart" (Prov. 21:2). This process of sifting strains out selfish or impure motives. I begin to delight myself in the Lord. The desires of my heart become conformed with his plans.

At this point, I am conscious of my need for the Holy Spirit's help. Just as the Holy Spirit led Paul on his missionary journeys, sending him to specific towns and people, he leads and

teaches us today. He is our sure and divine Guide who will steer us into God's truth. We can count on his enlightenment.

Once convinced that I am surrendered to God, that my motives are right, and that I have sought the Holy Spirit's help, I step out in obedience to the will of God as I perceive it. He can correct me or redirect me at any point—"wherever he pleases." I am trusting in him with all my heart and not leaning on my own understanding. I am his obedient child. God is fully responsible for those who fully commit themselves to him, and I know that he has taken me under his care and will not fail or forsake me.

Jesus, thank you that you desire that I know your will even more than I desire it. You are the Good Shepherd who guides his flock. I look to you as my Guide. Teach me the way in which I should go.

TOUCHSTONE

We need guidance, and we have the right Guide.

The sluggard says, "There is a lion outside!"
or, "I will be murdered in the streets!"

Proverbs 22:13

Excuses, Excuses

*W*hen we delay that important phone call, put off necessary chores around the house, postpone our medical examination, delay making things right with an offended friend, fail to spend time in the Word with the Lord, whatever our excuse, the truth is we are practicing the subtle art of procrastination.

Like the sluggard in Proverbs, we invent any number of excuses to delay crucial decisions or put off simple tasks. Nevertheless, procrastination is a form of bondage that is more costly than any of us would like to admit.

Some of us practice procrastination as a means of what I term "discomfort dodging." Our goal is not to feel bad, and we steadfastly avoid anything that has the potential of generating anxiety. We do not want to leave our comfort zone. When the apostle Paul presented the Gospel to Felix, a Roman governor, Felix "was afraid and said, 'That's enough for now! You may leave. When I find it convenient, I will send for you'" (Acts 24:25). Like Felix, we tend to postpone those circumstances that make us uneasy.

We also procrastinate because of a sense of inadequacy or a fear of failure. We might not succeed. We may very well blunder and embarrass ourselves; so why try in the first place? It is far easier to remain stationary and stay within our perceived capabilities than venture into risky endeavors. We doubt ourselves. As a result, important tasks are left undone; we deprive God of a vessel through which he desires to work. We experience nagging feelings of guilt, and our spiritual growth is stunted.

The first step for you to take if God is to deliver you from the bondage of procrastination is to admit your problem. Confess that you do make unnecessary excuses to avoid certain people or tasks. Once you admit you have the problem, ask God's forgiveness. He wants you to enjoy an abundant life and is willing to help you with any problem that hinders you from experiencing his fullness.

Then, by an act of faith, choose to live your life based on who you are in Christ Jesus rather than on your feelings of inadequacy or self-doubt. Believe that you *can* do all things through Christ who strengthens you for every task and makes you equal to every challenge (Phil. 4:13). Trust in the Lord with *all* your heart. He is your sufficiency. If you fail, move on and try and again. The truth is, you will find yourself succeeding far more than you imagined and discovering the reality of God's equipping power. The captivity of procrastination will be broken; and you will be able to face any situation with the sure knowledge that God is with you, for you, and in you. You are not on your own, and he will not fail you. Make this your motto: "Do it now."

Show me any areas of my life where I may be procrastinating and making excuses. Teach me to trust you and not look to my inadequate resources but to your abundant provision. Thank you for equipping me for every challenge.

TOUCHSTONE

Do it now!

Do not wear yourself out to get rich;
have the wisdom to show restraint.

Proverbs 23:4

Money Management

*M*oney is not primarily a financial issue for the Christian. Certainly, we are to live under budgetary constraints and use money wisely; but for the believer, money is fundamentally a spiritual issue. What matters is not how we view money but how God views it. When we approach it from his perspective, then the management of our finances is governed by spiritual principles, not cultural trends.

The bottom line for understanding money from a spiritual vantage point is this: God owns it all. It is God who created the heavens and the earth. It is God who created humankind. By right of creation, God is the sole owner of the universe and its enormous wealth. "'The silver is mine and the gold is mine,' declares the LORD Almighty" (Hag. 2:8). God gives us the health, wisdom, life, and strength to make money. While we may sharpen our skills through education, God provides us with all the raw material for accumulating income. Money is not evil. Wealth is not sinful. But whether we work for it, invest it, save it, or give it away, all our wealth belongs to the Lord Jesus Christ.

That puts the matter of our finances into an entirely new perspective. Since God is the sole owner of our resources, our responsibility is simply to manage what he entrusts to us. We are stewards of his riches. Our paycheck, our investments, our bank account—little or big—are to be administered under the guidance of practical scriptural principles.

God's Word tells us that poor managers of a little money will be poor managers of much money. If we are faithful in using our present treasures responsibly and obediently, God will entrust additional finances into our care. Faithfully handling your finances means you avoid the worldly snare of competing with others. It means that you are to be content with what God provides, concentrating on the very real rewards that come from being rich in good works. It means that giving God at least a tenth of your income will be a priority, not an option. It means

that you will do everything possible to avoid the debt trap and its bondage. There are hundreds of Scriptures that give God's viewpoint on money, and they will revolutionize the way you handle your finances.

Money will never satisfy completely. It was not meant to be an idol but merely a medium of exchange. It is not something we place our confidence in. Rather, our trust is wholly in God, who supplies all our needs according to his riches in glory.

Evaluating money from God's viewpoint will prevent us from squandering our time and talents on the relentless pursuit of wealth. It will liberate us instead to seek God's mind and wisdom and enjoy the superabundance of living by his unchanging, profitable principles.

I choose to pursue you, Lord, not wealth. Since you own it all, you will give me what I need as I depend on you. Let my finances be ordered by you and not by my impulses. I look forward to the freedom you will bring in this area as I obey you.

TOUCHSTONE

God owns it all.

By wisdom a house is built,
and through understanding it is established;
through knowledge its rooms are filled
with rare and beautiful treasures.

Proverbs 24:3–4

The House Built on the Rock

*T*he home is the greenhouse where godly wisdom is cultivated. The power of consistent Christian living in the context of family relationships is the primary spiritual classroom for authentic Christianity. The home is where the majority of behavioral traits—good and bad—are learned, reinforced, and passed along to future generations.

God's wisdom fills the home when acceptance of each member is faithfully practiced. Did you know that each member of your family, whether saved or not, is of great worth to God? All your family members have been created by him and are greatly loved by him. Their value is inestimable in his eyes, and he desires that everyone know him. Do you accept your mate, your children, your in-laws, your grandchildren just as they are, or do you love them only when they meet your performance standards? Paul wrote, "Accept one another, then, just as Christ accepted you" (Rom. 15:7). How does Christ accept you? Unconditionally. How should you accept the members of your family? In the same way.

A companion of acceptance is accountability to God. Parents must provide loving limits for their children, but every family member is ultimately accountable to God for his or her actions. Understanding and applying this truth teaches the children to seek to know God's mind and learn that their primary task is to obey him. Obeying mom and dad then becomes simply an expression of their desire to please and follow God. Husband and wife are freed from the bondage of selfish desires in order to rightly esteem one another.

A home is also filled with fragrant and appealing spiritual riches when each family member adopts a servant's spirit. Most family arguments and dissension stem from a failure to yield

personal rights. A person filled with the Spirit of Christ strongly desires to serve. He does not seek to establish his own emotional turf but freely edifies and encourages other family members through his servant spirit.

Practice these spiritual disciplines in your home. Accept other family members as they are and let God change them according to his plan for their lives. Be accountable to God and obey him. Serve one another gladly. As you do, your home will be a divine display of God's gentle and enduring wisdom.

Lord, how I want your peace and love to fill my home. I understand that I must accept others and allow you to change them. Forgive me for any selfishness and show me practical ways that your love can flow through me to my family. Thank you.

TOUCHSTONE

*Fill your house with the
treasure of wisdom.*

*Like a city whose walls are broken down
is a man who lacks self-control.*

Proverbs 25:28

Controlling Your Thoughts

*I*n ancient civilizations, the primary defense for cities was huge, imposing walls. Once the walls were surmounted, victory for the aggressor was virtually ensured.

The Scriptures compare a person without self-control to such a ravaged city. He is at the mercy of external forces, subject to double-mindedness. He is tossed to and fro by turbulent emotions and passions. His life is unstable and only occasionally fruitful.

The key to developing self-control with a spiritual emphasis is not more self-determination. It is not a doubling of efforts or better time management. The pivotal discipline for gaining godly self-control is the renewing of the mind. Like the ancient walls, the mind is the crucial defense mechanism. If it is broached by negative, critical, undisciplined thoughts, our behavior and our entire personality are adversely affected. We act out the way we perceive ourselves, the way we think. Our actions conform with our thinking. Right thinking is the first step toward right living.

We renew our minds and exhibit the godly fruit of self-control and other biblical traits by first understanding our position in Christ. Our position in Christ is our relationship with him. We have been crucified with him. We were buried with him and raised with him. We are now seated with him in the heavenly places. He is living on the inside of us through the Holy Spirit.

We can control our thinking, and thus our behavior, through the knowledge of our identity in Christ. We are new creatures, saints, holy and blameless in him. When Satan assaults the walls of our minds with alluring enticements, we do not have to yield, because of who we are in Christ. He is the source of our strength. He is our life.

Since Christ is now your life and you are in him, it makes

good sense to "set your [mind] on things above, not on earthly things" (Col. 3:2). Our thinking is in keeping with our position in Christ. We concentrate on the things that are true, right, pure, noble, lovely, admirable, praiseworthy, and excellent (Phil. 4:8). We view things from God's perspective.

"How can I do that?" you ask. Well, when I was young, people ordered many items from a catalog. They had never seen the items except as they were pictured in the catalog. The Scriptures are our catalog. We know what setting our minds on heavenly things is like because God's Word reveals his mind to us.

Does that mean we ignore our earthly responsibilities? Of course not. However, we seek God's kingdom first, allowing his priorities and his ways to saturate our thinking. We realize that we are here primarily to glorify him; and as we do, he promises to take care of our daily necessities, leading us into a more intimate walk with him as we go about our tasks.

The godly fruit of self-control comes as the Holy Spirit works by his power to renew our minds. It is then that our behavior is transformed.

I understand that my mind is a battleground, Lord. Only as you renew my mind can I win the war. Don't let me be led astray by feeling, but continually remind me of who I am in you.

TOUCHSTONE

The way you perceive yourself determines your actions.

As charcoal to embers and as wood to fire,
so is a quarrelsome man for kindling strife.

Proverbs 26:21

A Gentle Spirit

A man loves what God loves and hates what God hates. Although God hates all sin, he greatly detests the evil of spreading "dissension among brothers" (Prov. 6:19). God is opposed to all forms of quarreling and bickering—evils that spread hostility and anger.

The cure for strife is a gentle spirit. A gentle spirit is not feminine or masculine. It is a divinely given spirit, which pervades our hearts through the supernatural activity of the Holy Spirit. It is an inner adornment that should characterize every follower of Jesus Christ, the One who described himself as "gentle and humble in heart" (Matt. 11:29).

A gentle person is a peacemaker. He does not want peace at any cost, but he does nothing to unduly offend or disturb another. He speaks firmly and confidently but not arrogantly. He appreciates the worth of others as God's handiwork. His gentleness is revealed in his actions and his words. "A gentle answer turns away wrath, but a harsh word stirs up anger" (Prov. 15:1).

A gentle person is an effective tool in Christ's hand in almost every relationship. The gentle spouse shows the love of God to his or her mate. The gentle worker demonstrates the reality of Christ's compassion in a cold and harsh workplace. Even when others belligerently attack our faith in God, we are to respond clearly but with "gentleness and respect" (1 Peter 3:15). A godly, gentle spirit is a visible testimony of the character of God to believer and unbeliever alike.

Isn't it interesting that when God spoke to the prophet Elijah in the Old Testament, his voice was not dramatically loud. It was not in the mighty wind or the forceful earthquake that he revealed himself, but in the "gentle whisper" (1 Kings 19:12). God desires that we too speak in a gentle voice.

Ask Christ to fill you daily with the Holy Spirit. Rest in him. Abide in him. The divine sap of God's gentle Spirit will flow through you to others who desperately need the healing touch of God. You will avoid quarrels. You will not be obsessed with your own self-interests. You will be an attractive witness for Christ and sow the seeds of peace everywhere you go. What a wonderful harvest you will reap.

Lord, your gentleness was so evident as you ministered on earth. You were kind to all who sought your help. Through your Spirit implant in me your gentleness. Keep me away from strife and make me a peacemaker.

TOUCHSTONE

Christ in you is the gentle Lamb of God.

The crucible for silver and the furnace for gold,
but man is tested by the praise he receives.

Proverbs 27:21

The Test of Success

*S*uccess can be just as much of a spiritual proving ground as adversity. In fact, many who endure the darkness of trials fail in the glow of success. God uses our response to the praises of others to reveal and expose the bent of our hearts.

Handling success properly begins with a right estimation of ourselves. God is the source of all our talents and energies. The glory is his. But we are his instruments, his workmanship. When our deeds earn the approval of others, we can be gracious and thankful. There is no need for false humility.

The apostle Paul put it this way: "Do not think of yourself more highly than you ought, but rather think of yourself with sober judgment, in accordance with the measure of faith God has given you" (Rom. 12:3). We are not worms. We are not simpletons. God has given each of us a sound mind and equipped us to honor him in our appointed tasks. We can humbly receive the appreciation of others while still acknowledging God.

Paul understood the tension that personal praise can bring. When God used Paul to heal a lame man, the people began to worship him. However, Paul pointed their attention to the true God. In Corinth, Paul put out another fire of personal adulation when he discovered that some of the Corinthians were following him rather than Christ.

The subtle appeal of success is always to enlarge our self-esteem and magnify our importance. Notice that I said "enlarge" and "magnify." A person with proper self-esteem rightly values his own worth as God's handiwork but realizes the awesome power and majesty of his Maker. Any praise that is accorded him only serves to stimulate his worship of such a magnificent Father.

When others publicly notice you, receive their appreciation and then take a few moments in private to thank our heavenly Father. That is what Jesus did. After he performed several of his miracles and the crowds gathered, he withdrew for a season of private fellowship with the heavenly Father.

Make sure that you do not praise or exalt yourself. "Let another praise you, and not your own mouth" (Prov. 27:2). Accept the congratulations of others, give glory to God, keep your eyes on your Source—Jesus Christ—and you will pass the test of praise.

Heavenly Father, I enjoy success, but do not let it draw me away from you. Keep my focus right so that when others praise me, I can receive their approval without expanding my ego. Keep me alert to the dangers of success by keeping me close to you.

TOUCHSTONE

Seek to please God, and the praise of others will be kept in proper perspective.

The righteous are as bold as a lion.

Proverbs 28:1

Gaining Confidence

*A*re you a confident Christian? Is your relationship with Jesus Christ characterized by a growing boldness, or are you somewhat tentative and timid? While the believer is to walk humbly before God, he should also express great confidence in his great God.

We can be confident in the purpose of God. His purpose is to conform us to the image of his Son, Jesus Christ; and he *will* finish that objective. We can be "confident of this, that he who began a good work in [us] will carry it on to completion until the day of Christ Jesus" (Phil. 1:6). As we cooperate with the Father on earth, we are transformed into his image. The comforting news is that he accomplishes this by his Spirit and by his grace. We are not left to our own devices or cleverness. In heaven the job will be finished, for God always completes what he begins.

We can be confident in presenting our petitions to the Father. We are to come boldly into God's presence and there present our needs and burdens. He promises that he will hear and answer us according to his love and wisdom. The shed blood of Jesus Christ has paved our way into the throne room of God. We need not be afraid, for he is our Friend. We need not feel guilty, for all our sins are forgiven. We come to a throne of mercy and grace. When we ask according to his will, he assures us that we will receive his gracious and timely reply. "This is the confidence we have in approaching God: that if we ask anything according to his will, he hears us. And if we know that he hears us—whatever we ask—we know that we have what we asked of him" (1 John 5:14–15).

Our confidence is also in the promises of God. God's Word is living and powerful. Peter wrote that God "has given us his very great and precious promises, so that through them you may participate in the divine nature" (2 Peter 1:4). The Scriptures are God's very personal word to you. You can count on a promise from God. He will fulfill his Word in his way, in his timing; he

always keeps his promises. When you place your faith in the truths of the Scriptures, you will never be disappointed. Each time you trust in his Word you experience the reality of his truth.

If you are lacking confidence, ponder these truths. They will encourage you, sustain you, and strengthen your inner self. You will mount up on eagles' wings and face life with great assurance in the incredible goodness of God.

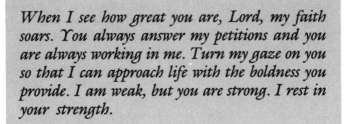

When I see how great you are, Lord, my faith soars. You always answer my petitions and you are always working in me. Turn my gaze on you so that I can approach life with the boldness you provide. I am weak, but you are strong. I rest in your strength.

TOUCHSTONE

*The more we magnify God,
the smaller our problems
appear.*

Fear of man will prove to be a snare,
but whoever trusts in the Lord is kept safe.
Proverbs 29:25

Pulling Down Strongholds

*F*ear is a major stronghold in the hearts of many Christians. I talk with people who are afraid of so many things— afraid of losing control, afraid of the future, afraid of other people. Some live in a constant state of worry.

The antidote for fear is a fixed focus of faith on the Person of Jesus Christ. As long as we dwell on anxious circumstances, turning them constantly over in our minds, we will likely remain in emotional turmoil. However, when we choose—and it is an act of the will—to focus on Jesus Christ, our fearful feelings can and will gradually diminish.

That may sound too easy. I do not want to make light of your fears, for they are very real. Nonetheless, I want to encourage you to place your trust in Jesus Christ. It is really the only means to put your fears in perspective and pull down the strongholds of anxiety.

You can overcome your fears because God *knows* about your circumstances. He is not distant or far off. He is in you, so he is keenly aware of the factors that generate fear. Peace can begin to replace fear when you realize that the God of heaven and earth is intimately aware of your needs and problems.

It is comforting to understand that God knows about our fears, but it is even more encouraging to grasp that he *cares*. Jesus Christ is your personal Shepherd who cares for his flock. Night and day he works to administer his love, grace, mercy, and help to you. He loves you. He delights in you. He wanted to share his life with you so much that he came to earth and died in your place. That is how much he cares. He will spare nothing to aid you. He will withhold no good thing from you.

Not only is God aware of your fears and concerned for your well-being, but he is also *able* to bring about change. God is in

125

control. There is no situation that he cannot handle. There is no circumstance producing fear that he is not able to work out for your welfare. The power of God is available to help you. There is nothing too difficult for him.

God knows. God cares. God is able. Put all of your trust in Jesus Christ. Tell him about your fears and then choose to place your focus and faith in the loving hands of your loving God.

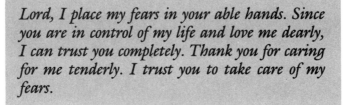

Lord, I place my fears in your able hands. Since you are in control of my life and love me dearly, I can trust you completely. Thank you for caring for me tenderly. I trust you to take care of my fears.

TOUCHSTONE

Remove fear with a fixed focus of faith on Jesus Christ.

Ants are creatures of little strength,
yet they store up their food in the summer.

Proverbs 30:25

What Are You Living For?

I often find that people with limited resources or time can accomplish far more than individuals with far greater talents. The key to their achievements in most cases is diligent planning. Planning is simply making preparations today for tomorrow's opportunities.

When we read the New Testament, it becomes obvious that the apostle Paul had a distinct plan for spreading the Gospel. He visited the leading cities of various provinces, realizing that the Gospel's influence would spread to other communities. It is likewise apparent that God had a plan of salvation, the plan to send his Son to die for our sins. He conceived this plan even before the creation of the universe.

The key to good planning is good goal setting. Goals are written, clearly understood objectives that we arrive at after careful thought and prayer. The only really rewarding goal setting comes after we have asked God to search our hearts for any improper motives and surrendered our wills to his. Once we do these things, we are free to establish goals that are measurable, honest, reasonable, and clear. Ask yourself the following questions: "Can I honestly ask God's help in striving to reach this goal?" "Will it help someone else reach his or her goal?" "Will it violate my conscience?" "Am I willing to pay the price to succeed?"

You will find this process easier if you divide your goals for various sectors of your life—spiritual, family, vocational, and social. Write down as many goals as you feel are necessary. Ask God for discernment as to which goals may not be according to his will. Be flexible and review your goals from time to time, making adjustments as God guides. You may find that you understated your goals in some areas and overstated them in others.

Many years ago my wife and I spent a week setting goals for our personal life, the family, and our ministry. I can honestly say that week was one of the most important of my life. God gave me a tiny glimpse of what our future could hold if we would only trust him and follow the plan he was giving us. I have seen God fulfill many of these goals ahead of my expected schedule and in the most remarkable ways. Most important, my faith in God has grown by leaps and bounds. I now understand more clearly what an awesome God we serve.

As you pray and plan, setting goals under God's leadership, your faith will also grow and you will be used to the maximum of your potential.

Lord, I desire to accomplish your will. I understand that setting goals is a realistic way for me to achieve your purposes. I choose to set aside the time to pray and think about your objectives for my life. I am trusting you to enable me to reach my potential.

TOUCHSTONE

Set your goals and live by faith.

Charm is deceptive, and beauty is fleeting;
but a woman who fears the Lord is to be praised.
                                                    Proverbs 31:30

A Virtuous Woman

A godly woman is a great treasure. She is a gift from the Lord and is to be received and treated with great dignity. The description of the virtuous woman in Proverbs 31 is one of the most beautiful descriptions of womankind in all of literature.

The most important aspect of the godly woman is her character: "A wife of noble character who can find?" (Prov. 31:10). Our culture concentrates on physical appearance. We are more interested in how a woman looks or dresses than in what kind of person she is. The Bible teaches a far different assessment of a woman's worth. It is the inner beauty of the godly woman that makes her so valuable.

Her character is displayed most vividly as she cares for her household. She is diligent and thrifty, providing for the needs of her husband and children. Such provision is the motivation for her work, whether it is in the home or on the job. Her speech also reveals her worth. Her communication with husband, children, and friends is encouraging and instructive. She realizes the importance of well-chosen words and their influence on her family.

She is vital to the success of the family. Her husband should be fully aware of that. He should also take time to understand her needs and meet them appropriately. She is to be treated as his spiritual equal. He is to love her in the same way that Christ loves the church—unconditionally, sacrificially, and wholeheartedly. So crucial is the relationship between a husband and his wife that his own prayers to God can be hindered if he treats her unfairly. Could anything shout her value to God more clearly?

Her children are to respect her and appreciate the many sacrifices she makes on their behalf. Their obedience to her is a demonstration of her importance and an acknowledgment of her spiritual wisdom.

A home, a community, a nation cannot function under God without the noble efforts of the godly woman. She is a unique temple of the Holy Spirit and reflects the character of God in an unrivaled way. "Give her the reward she has earned, and let her works bring her praise at the city gate" (Prov. 31:31). Express your appreciation for her with verbal praise and loving deeds.

A godly woman is a treasure that should adorn every Christian home.

Father, thank you for making each of us so special. You have made woman to be cherished and treasured. Thank you for the example in the Scriptures of godly women who display your character.

TOUCHSTONE

A godly woman is a heavenly gift.

A Touch of His Peace

Contents

Photographs

Introduction

One of the most comforting passages of Scripture is Jesus' discourse with his disciples in John 13–17. Jesus intimately shares his impending betrayal, arrest, death, and ascension to the Father.

The disciples are worried, puzzled, perplexed. What will they do when Jesus is gone?

In their distress, Jesus speaks these soothing words: "Peace I leave with you; my peace I give you. I do not give to you as the world gives. Do not let your hearts be troubled and do not be afraid" (John 14:27).

Jesus' words of comfort are for us today as well. In our hour of pain, confusion, or fear, we can experience a supernatural peace that steadies and sustains our fretful spirit. Innermost peace is given only by God. While others promise peace, Jesus himself is our peace who lives in us.

Our circumstances may seem intolerable. Our challenges may appear insurmountable. Our obstacles may breed constant, unremitting worry and turmoil. Yet in the midst of our conflicts, Jesus gives us his perfect peace if we will but receive it. It is his to give; and he has chosen to freely extend it to you.

Jesus stills a distraught heart. He calms an anxious mind. He gives rest to the weary and brings blessed refreshment, renewal, and contentment. The God of peace is with you and for you. He is at home in your heart through the presence of the Comforter, the Holy Spirit.

You can consistently experience Christ's peace in every circumstance. He will never leave or forsake you. He will never leave you helpless or hopeless.

It is my prayer that these devotionals will bring a touch of his peace to your life. God does not always take away trouble, but he can and does heal a troubled heart. His peace "transcends all understanding" (Phil. 4:7).

A Touch of His Peace

But now in Christ Jesus you who once were far away have been brought near through the blood of Christ. For he himself is our peace.

Ephesians 2:13–14

Peace with God

The earthquake that shook San Francisco in 1989 did considerable damage to bridges and highways. However, residential destruction was limited primarily to an area along the bay. The ruin was not due to poor construction or proximity to the epicenter of the quake. It occurred because the homes were constructed on land reclaimed from the bay: when the quake struck, the precarious foundation gave way.

In order for peace to endure, it must have an authentic foundation. Our remedies for global, relational, and personal peace are too often built on faulty premises, relying on flawed practices and people to achieve and maintain it.

This was the case for the rebellious people of Jeremiah's day. Mired in greed, guile, and corruption, the priests and prophets promised an artificially contrived peace: "They dress the wound of my people as though it were not serious. 'Peace, peace,' they say, when there is no peace" (Jer. 6:14).

The superficial prescriptions for peace in a world of turmoil will not work apart from a spiritual cornerstone. There is no peace for the wicked, unbelieving person, because God's wrath opposes him. He walks under the sentence of eternal death and burdensome guilt. God and the unrepentant are foes, not friends; and though there may be moments or seasons of peace, the enmity and judgment of God hang over the head and heart of those who do not believe. They are at war with God and strangers to real peace. Death holds nothing but grim punishment and agony for them for eternity.

God has laid the solid foundation for true peace through the Cross of his Son, Jesus Christ. On the tree Jesus shouldered the full fury of the holy God against sin and paved the way through his death for everlasting peace with the Father. The instant you place your trust in Christ for the forgiveness of sin,

you are reconciled to God. The rebellion is over. The conflict has ended. You have been reconciled to God who has made "peace through his blood, shed on the cross" (Col. 1:20).

Because you now have peace *with* God, you can experience the fathomless peace *of* God. You cannot reverse the order. As long as one is God's enemy, enduring peace is unattainable. But once a person looks to the Cross and receives its merits by faith, the peace of God is forever his.

When Christ returns to establish his kingdom on earth, peace will reign universally. Until then, the Christian has the awesome privilege of experiencing and extending the peace of Christ. Still more, he has entered into a personal relationship with Christ marked by a supernatural peace the world cannot duplicate. The right foundation has been laid. Whatever shakes your life may temporarily unsettle you, but it can never disturb your everlasting relationship with the Prince of Peace.

Heavenly Father, I realize that sin has created strife and enmity between you and me. I thank you that Christ's death on the cross satisfied your holy wrath and reconciled me to yourself. Thank you for taking this initiative, Father. I never could have settled the conflict in my own knowledge. You have given me peace that is sure, everlasting, and unfading. You are for me, not against me, and that is cause for unceasing praise and thanksgiving.

TOUCHSTONE

No God, no peace.
Know God, know peace.

Find rest, O my soul, in God alone; my hope comes from him.
Psalm 62:5

Rest for the Weary

The Bible is a book of paradoxes. If we want to live, we must die to self. If we want to achieve greatness, we must humble ourselves and become servants. If we desire to receive, we must first give.

Perhaps one of the strangest paradoxes is found in the book of Hebrews. The author tells the enticing news about entering what he calls a "Sabbath-rest for the people of God" (Heb. 4:9). Just as God rested from his work of creation, so there exists a spiritual state of rest and refreshment for the weary and parched soul of the believer.

What wonderful news! The struggle does not have to be unending. The burden can be laid down. The walk of faith does not have to wear out our souls. But exactly how do we experience this profound rest? Here again is the paradox: "Let us, therefore, make every effort to enter that rest" (Heb. 4:11).

Rest is experienced through diligent effort and vigilance. It seems contradictory, doesn't it? It is the last thing the worn spiritual pilgrim wants to hear. He is at the end of his rope; how is it possible for him to work harder to find divine restoration?

The writer of Hebrews is not at odds with himself, nor is he in conflict with the biblical principle of rest. Rather, he is prescribing the exact remedy for enjoying the abundant Christian life in an entirely new dimension.

Here is the key: "For anyone who enters God's rest also rests from his own work, just as God did from his" (Heb. 4:10).

You are to rest from trying to make yourself acceptable to God. You are as righteous and acceptable in God's eyes today as you will be when you enter his very presence in heaven. God treats you today and forever according to the merits and mediation of the Cross, not your behavior. You are already pleasing to

God. You are already holy and blameless in his eyes. Your actions may not always measure up to your identity, but you are a child of God forever. You can cease from any works of self-righteousness.

We are to rest also from working in the energy of the flesh and live in the energy of the Holy Spirit. Living and working in the strength and power of your talents and abilities will only take you so far. It is a long, uphill climb that leads to eventual exhaustion and burnout.

But living according to the Spirit will bring you into the green pastures and beside the still waters of the Good Shepherd. "For it is God who works in you to will and to act according to his good purpose" (Phil. 2:13). That takes the strain off, doesn't it? That infuses the very power of God into your every thought, word, and deed. God is responsible for you. He saved you. He will sanctify you. He began a good work in you. He will complete it. Surely you are to obey, but you have the power of God to accomplish all that he has planned for your life. Forget manipulation. Reject clever plans. Cease from your own futile efforts to imitate Christ. Enter the rest of God by placing your trust in the finished work of the Cross. Commit your way to him. This is the way of success, endurance, and cherished rest for your innermost being. It is the rest of confident faith in the faithfulness of God.

O Lord, I see that I cannot enter into your peace and rest apart from abandoning all works of self-righteousness. I thank you that I do not have to make myself acceptable to you, for you have already made me acceptable. I gladly yield to the life of the Spirit, allowing him to flow through me. I have come to abide in Christ now, so that his inexhaustible strength may saturate me and flow through me.

TOUCHSTONE

When we come to the end
of ourselves, we are ready
to enter God's rest.

But the [Helper], the Holy Spirit, whom the Father will send in my name, will teach you all things.

John 14:26

The Helper

Jesus was the ultimate realist. Although he spoke often of the abundant life and the blessings of obedience, he never soft-pedaled the opposition, affliction, and suffering each believer would encounter.

Shortly before his death, he reminded his disciples of the rough road ahead of them. He knew the obstacles they would face as they spread the good news of salvation: "I have told you these things, so that in me you may have peace. In this world you will have trouble. But take heart! I have overcome the world" (John 16:33).

When you became a Christian, you began an exciting relationship with Christ; but it did not mean the end of your problems. More than likely, you have discovered intense struggles with temptations, tests, and trials that are an inevitable part of the Christian's road to maturity.

But you can "take heart," for you do have supernatural help in your spiritual journey. Jesus' words of warning were couched in the promise that he would send the Holy Spirit to aid the believer.

Jesus gives you his prevailing peace by giving you his all-sufficient Spirit. The power and person of the Spirit of God indwell you unceasingly. Whatever difficulties you face, the Holy Spirit is ever present to extend the peace of God to your heart and mind.

The Spirit of God will teach you in your perplexity. He is the author of the Scriptures and makes your soul susceptible to the calming reality of God's truth. He will teach you all you need to know, granting wisdom and knowledge for successful living. On many occasions, the Holy Spirit has revealed to me the right solutions to problems that I could not solve in my own strength.

The Spirit of God will guide you in your confusion. You do not know what lies ahead. In fact, you don't know what will happen in the very next minute. But the Holy Spirit does. He can guide you unerringly in his ways if you are willing to wait on him and accept his counsel.

The Spirit of God will comfort you in your heartache. Grief and loss are part of the human existence. The Holy Spirit tenderly sustains and upholds you in such seasons. The Greek word for the designation of the Holy Spirit as Counselor is *parakletos*, that is, "one called alongside to help and aid." What a marvelous description of the One whom God gives to us to experience his transcendent peace.

Jesus overcame the world by triumphing over every temptation, defeating the devil, and becoming obedient even to the point of death. This same Jesus lives in you today through the Holy Spirit who extends the precious peace of God to you at every turn. The Holy Spirit is God's gift of peace to you.

Lord, I do admit that at times I feel devoid of your peace. But it is not so, because your Spirit lives in me. Teach me to depend on you for your help. Make me aware of the Spirit's constant presence. Thank you, Holy Spirit, that you are willing to give me God's peace in any circumstance. I receive it gratefully. Sustain me with your peace.

TOUCHSTONE

The Helper is with you,
for you, and in you.

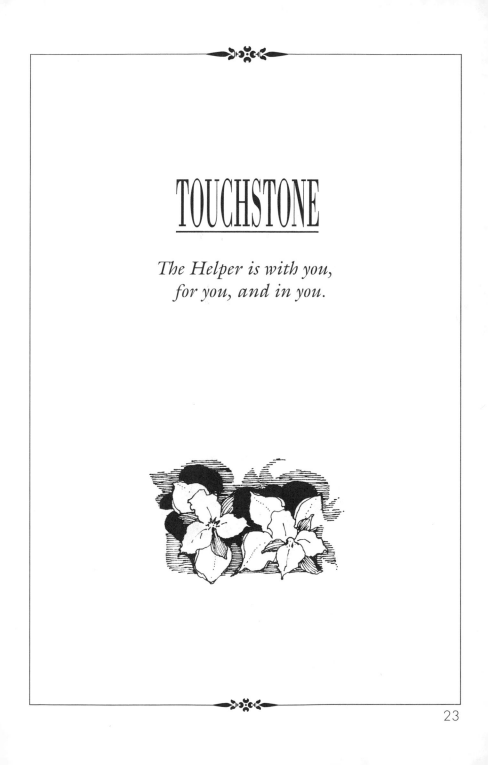

Without warning, a furious storm came up on the lake, so that the waves swept over the boat.

Matthew 8:24

When the Storms Come

I never paid much attention to hurricane reports until I pastored a church in Florida. Each fall the watch began for climatic disturbances that could eventually result in a full-scale hurricane with surging tides and destructive winds.

A hurricane did not strike my home; but I did learn a lot about them, including the mysterious "eye of the storm," an uncanny center of calm in the midst of fury.

The disciples once found themselves in a violent storm on the Sea of Galilee. The waves washed into the boat, the winds wailed, and the disciples feared for their lives. A weary and sleeping Jesus was awakened by his panic-stricken followers. He then demonstrated his deity by rebuking the turbulent winds and turning chaos into calm.

You may be in such a storm. It could be emotional, financial, or physical. It may be in your marriage or in your job. Like the disciples, you may be afraid and wonder where God is.

Know this: As there is calm in the eye of the storm, so there can be calm in the midst of your problem, because Jesus is at the center of your life. He is not asleep. He is not immune to your pain, for he himself has suffered the deep pain of the human lot.

He is on board with you and capable of demonstrating his magnificent deity to you in a myriad of ways. This is the truth that brings peace to your soul and calm to your emotions. This is the anchor that holds you in place when everything else seems to pull you loose from your moorings.

You are hand in hand with him in the storm, and you have his presence at the core of your life. There he can bring his

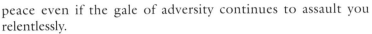

peace even if the gale of adversity continues to assault you relentlessly.

The apostle Paul wrote that the mystery of the gospel that has been made known is "Christ in you, the hope of glory" (Col. 1:27). Christ may calm the storm by removing the problem, or he will calm you as you go through the tempest. He is at the center of your life to reveal himself in new and majestic ways so that you may worship him and thank him.

Jesus is Immanuel—God with us. Though he may seem silent at times, he is never still. Though he may seem absent, he is always present. Though he may seem uncaring, he is positioning you for his greatest blessing.

Jesus is in the storm with you and capable of doing the impossible. That is your "hope of glory" and the cornerstone of peace for any storm.

Lord, I am caught off guard sometimes by unexpected problems. I find peace so elusive. I cannot get my mind off my problems. Help me to turn to you and know that you can quiet my storms with promises from your Word, with an assuring touch of your Spirit. I am so grateful you are with me in the storms.

TOUCHSTONE

*Whatever is at the center
of your life determines
your course.*

When Peter came to Antioch, I opposed him to his face, because he was clearly in the wrong.

Galatians 2:11

Caring Enough to Confront

The way of peace is not always the path of least resistance. On occasion, the means of establishing peace is confrontation. It is not a popular choice, and it certainly should not be the standard one. However, when a problem between people reaches the boiling point or when you witness continued injustice and inequity in a particular circumstance, confrontation may be the solution.

Paul was forced to choose that option to deal with Peter's hypocrisy. The acknowledged leader of the disciples, Peter was afraid of Jewish opinion regarding his relationship with the Gentiles. He timidly appeased the Jewish Christians by withdrawing from Gentile fellowship upon Paul's visit. His errant behavior was drawing Jewish believers into legalism, and Paul bluntly rebuked him.

When confrontation is necessary, it must be accomplished in a biblical framework and for biblical purposes. Your motivation must be pure. That means you must spend considerable time in prayer, asking God to cleanse you from selfish considerations. God is concerned with the heart; and if confrontation serves only to vent your anger, then you are not approaching the problem God's way.

Confrontation should be reserved for situations that involve a clear violation of biblical principle or spiritual standard of conduct. There will always be people of different temperaments who annoy us or circumstances that irritate us. These are best accepted as God's chisels for conforming us to his image: "A man's wisdom gives him patience; it is to his glory to overlook an offense" (Prov. 19:11).

The goal of confrontation should be correction, not condemnation. As God's ambassadors, we are called to reconcile, helping to heal and mend broken relationships. If we confront someone whose behavior is plainly and consistently wrong, our objective should be to guide him to the truth that sets him free, not to vindicate ourselves. We must do all of this in the context of gentleness and kindness, realizing that this is the way God deals with us in our disobedience.

Keep your confrontation on the personal and private level. Do it as Paul did, "face to face." Keep it strictly between you and the offending person. Don't unwisely share the problem with friends in an attempt to find support. If confrontation succeeds in solving the problem, peace will supplant the reign of tension. If it doesn't succeed, leave the matter with God and the results in his capable hands.

I do not like confrontation, Lord; and when I do think about a need to confront, I usually get angry. Give me the courage I need to confront the problem your way, always remembering the undeserved love you shower on me despite my erratic behavior. I ask for your wisdom to help me know when to confront someone and when to remain silent. Thank you that your goal is peace and that I can count on your guidance.

TOUCHSTONE

*Confrontation sometimes is
God's hard road to a
peaceful destination.*

He has given us new birth into a living hope through the resur-
rection of Jesus Christ from the dead, and into an inheritance
that can never perish, spoil, or fade—kept in heaven for you.
1 Peter 1:3–4

Saved and Sure

I have counseled people in many distressing situations, but I cannot think of any worse predicament than that of the people who are unsure of their eternal security. For such, the Christian life is an unsteady tightrope, precariously walked by good works. Any stumble, and their eternal destiny is in doubt.

I cannot think of anything that causes more misery. Such people have no semblance of peace, only intense agony over whether or not they have lived up to God's standard. They have only a hope of heaven, no guarantee.

This kind of living is treacherous and, when examined, is shown to be wholly derived from false teaching and erroneous thinking. If your eternal security is directly coupled with your good works, then how good must you be? How good is good enough? How do you know whether you have passed the test or not? What happens if you die on a bad day?

Can you see the fallacy and confusion this kind of theology breeds? Yet multitudes—and that is probably an underestimation—are caught in its bewildering web. All one needs is a heart open to the truth of Scripture and the power of the Cross to be set free and know peace in an entirely new dimension.

God's standard is perfection. Now, how do you live up to that? It is impossible; and that is precisely why God sent his perfect Son to be our substitutionary, all-sufficient atoning sacrifice at Calvary. Christianity is a liberating faith; and Jesus Christ is our Deliverer, bearing our sin along with its penalty—death—and providing full forgiveness of our sin by faith in his person and work.

You are saved by grace through faith in Christ and kept for all eternity by grace through faith in Christ. Good works do matter for the Christian, but for the purpose of rewards in heaven, not as a means to escape judgment. Once you believe, you can never be condemned again, never judged again for your sins. Jesus was condemned and judged on Calvary by God, once and for all.

You can know the peace that eternal security in Christ brings as you accept the truth that you are saved and kept by Christ's performance, not yours. You cannot fall from grace, because salvation is but an introduction into a life of grace that never ends (Rom. 5:1–2). Your eternal security has been won and is preserved by Jesus Christ, not your works. Once you are saved, nothing can loosen God's eternal grip on you. You are forever forgiven and assured of heaven because Jesus now lives in you; his Spirit is the down payment for what is to come.

Your eternal security is rooted in Christ. He saved you. He keeps you. He has prepared a place for you in heaven. You have a firm reservation that no sin can cancel. Accept this truth and exchange the misery of self-righteousness for the joy of being in the righteousness of God in Christ. You are eternally secure in Christ.

Father, how liberating it is to know that my eternal security is in your hands, not mine. Once a saint, I am always a saint. Nothing can change that, and nothing can take away my home in heaven. It is Christ's work of forgiveness and indwelling life that makes my eternal security firm. Thank you for the remarkable peace this truth brings.

TOUCHSTONE

*You can never fall from
grace when it is God
who keeps you.*

God is our refuge and strength, an ever-present help in trouble.
Psalm 46:1

The Hiding Place

You have a refuge, a stronghold, a fortress to which you may come for stability and calm when life's pressures mount and your inner peace quivers. During his wilderness exile the psalmist David used this vivid imagery more than any other Scripture writer. God, not the numerous caves and caverns of the desert mountains, was his true shelter. Jehovah God kept him, protected him, and sustained him physically, spiritually, and emotionally.

Christ is the believer's refuge, the Person to whom we may come with every complaint and dilemma. The Old Testament speaks of dwelling in the "shelter of his wings" (Ps. 61:4), referring to the nearness and protection of the heavenly Father in times of trouble. Can anything or anyone really permanently harm us when God is our shield? If Jesus is the defense of our life, we will not cower before people or circumstances. If God is for us, who can be against us?

How do we make Christ our refuge? How do we come to that place of knowing that he is responsible for our safekeeping? The writer of Proverbs gives us one clue: "The name of the LORD is a strong tower; the righteous run to it and are safe" (Prov. 18:10).

He is El Shaddai, the Almighty God. This name literally means the All-Sufficient One or the All-Bountiful One. He fulfills every promise of Scripture and is faithful to perform his Word. He is El Elyon, the Most High God, who rules over people and nations and whose strength and power no one can resist. He is your impenetrable shield and your protector. He is El Olam, the Everlasting One, the God who is eternally consistent. He is the stability of your life when things seem to unravel. He is El Roi, the God who sees. He watches over you, seeing and knowing all that happens, and he comes to your aid.

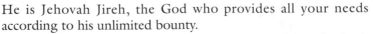

He is Jehovah Jireh, the God who provides all your needs according to his unlimited bounty.

The names of God, and there are many, tell us who he is and how he acts. They are the reflection of his attributes and character—his love, grace, mercy, kindness, goodness, faithfulness, gentleness. This is the God to whom you may run for refuge, to whom you may go for shelter and help. The problems may not subside; but when you make God your hiding place, you may confidently face the day secure in his provision, help, and protection.

God is our refuge also as we come to him in heartfelt honesty with our needs: "Trust in him at all times, O people; pour out your hearts to him, for God is our refuge" (Ps. 62:8). Turning to Christ and releasing our fears and anxieties in earnest prayer is a powerful step into the refuge of the everlasting arms.

Lord, I want to know you better so that I may trust you more. You really are my refuge and stronghold. Teach me to run to you quickly so that I may find shelter in your everlasting arms. There I know I am safe.

TOUCHSTONE

*The shadow of the Almighty
is large enough to
encompass every need.*

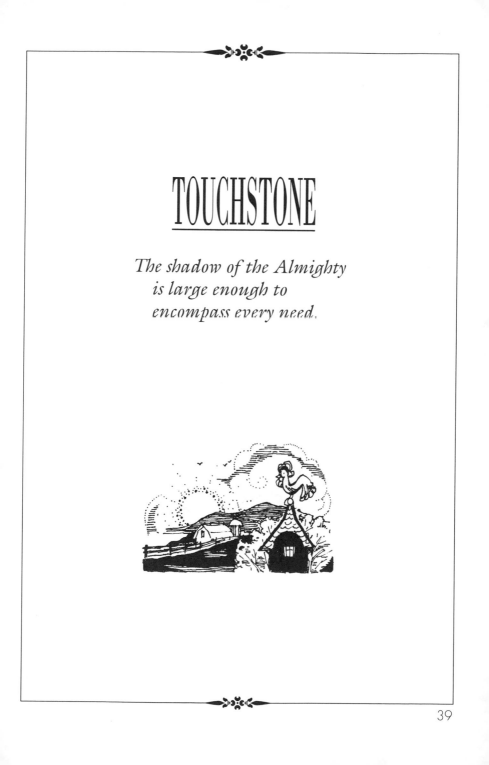

*The grass withers and the flowers fall, but the word of our **God** stands forever.*

Isaiah 40:8

Passing Feelings

Picture this scene in your mind: You are out on a boat in the middle of a placid lake. It's fall, and the leaves are a crayon box full of colors. Canadian geese fly overhead. After slowly rowing on the lake for an hour, you return to the dock that is connected to a cabin on the shore. You sip a mug of hot chocolate and sit on the porch rocker as the sun fades.

Now imagine this scene: You are stuck in the middle of bumper-to-bumper traffic on the interstate. You are already late for work. Sirens scream as they rush by on the shoulder to reach the wreck a few hundred feet in front of you. Impatient drivers surround you. Your cup of hot coffee spills on your lap as you hit the brakes to avoid rear-ending the car in front of you.

If you recorded your emotional response in these instances, your feelings would differ widely. The first setting evokes feelings of serenity, whereas the second ignites flashes of anger and irritability.

Feelings rush in and out. They rise and fall with circumstances and are invariably hinged to the thermometer of our emotions. We know what it is like to be flushed with anger one hour and smiling the next. Emotions are part of our personality and are God-given, but they were not bestowed on us as reliable spiritual gauges. Housed in a body of sin and subject to a variety of external influences, they are false props for the genuine peace of God.

God's peace is anchored to his Word, not our feelings. The unchanging revelation of Scripture is our accurate and predictable guide for authentic, godly peace. God's Word is eternal fact, everlasting truth that can be counted on regardless of our emotions.

We may feel hopeless. God's Word says our hope is sure and certain and can never be taken away. We may feel powerless, but God's Word says we have all the strength we need in him. We may feel lonely, but God's Word says he is always with us. We may feel we cannot approach God, but his Word says we have free access to him through his Son, Jesus Christ.

Decide now that you will not let your feelings dictate your awareness and experience of God's peace. Lean your whole weight upon the truth of God's Word and refuse to be shaken. Only in this way can darkness become light, doubt become faith, and despair become confident hope. Don't suppress your emotions, but let them lead you to the Rock of God's truth. That is what standing on the Word is all about. God will not let you fall.

I realize my feelings are not totally reliable gauges for experiencing your peace, Lord. How thankful I am that you never change and that you steady me with your peace as I learn to depend on your truth. I submit my emotions to you and ask you to keep them under the reign of your abiding peace.

TOUCHSTONE

The peace of God is hinged on his Word, not on my emotions.

And my God will meet all your needs according to his glorious riches in Christ Jesus.

Philippians 4:19

Unmet Needs

A well-known Christian author and thinker once said, "Mankind is one vast need." What an apt description of the human lot. As long as our needs—emotional, spiritual, physical, material—are being met, we are relatively happy. But when one or more of our needs is unfilled, peace is a scarce commodity.

Learning to deal with such unmet needs while maintaining a positive faith is a critical step in experiencing the kind of contentment that Christ promises us for every circumstance. That learning process begins by realizing that Jesus understands our needs and has the power to meet them. In his humanity, Christ participated in the full scope of human existence, including needs. He was hungry. He was thirsty. He needed rest. He endured agony of soul before his death. And now, having suffered all of that, he feels for us. He hurts for us. He knows our needs.

"But if God knows my needs and can meet them, why hasn't he?" As a pastor, I have heard that question many times from singles who yearn to be married, from the unemployed who only want a decent job, from wives who long for their husbands to tenderly communicate love to them.

In a way, all of these are expressions of man's three basic needs—a sense of belonging, a sense of competence, and a sense of worth. These are the deepest emotional and spiritual needs of the soul; and when they are unmet, they create the most intense pain.

Yet, if we have a genuine need (as distinguished from an illegitimate desire) that is not met, we must look at several things. Have we been willfully disobedient to God in some area? Are we refusing to wait on God to meet our needs in his way and in his time? Are we wrongfully manipulating people or circumstances? Is our motivation misdirected? Is God trying to

teach us something? Is God calling us to repentance or leading us to trust him in a greater way?

During the delay—the time between when you have asked God to meet a need and the time he supplies that need—you must refuse every false means of satisfying your need. There will be the temptation to seek to meet your needs in your way, in your timing. Yielding to temptation may superficially and temporarily meet your need, but it will not last. The consequences will create only more frustration.

The only Person who can satisfy all your needs is Jesus Christ. Because of the Cross, where you were reconciled to God, you are of great value to him, you belong to him, and you are accepted by him. An intimate relationship with Jesus Christ is really the only enduring means to meet all of your needs. You can never exhaust the reservoir of his grace, mercy, and love for you.

God will meet your needs according to his good will. It may take time. The means and end may not be what you anticipated. But if you will seek to find your deepest needs met through your friendship with Christ, you will truly discover that God does indeed supply every need according to his superabundant riches. Jesus never fails.

How often I have looked to someone or something else to meet my needs, Lord. I realize this is tempting but futile. Help me to accept the truth that you are the only One who can truly satisfy my innermost longings. I turn to you now and ask that you will meet my needs in your way. I know that you only want my best, so I submit all to you.

TOUCHSTONE

*When you have Christ, you
have everything you need.*

*You will keep in perfect peace him whose mind is steadfast,
because he trusts in you.*

Isaiah 26:3

The Right Focus

A large portrait of Daniel in the lion's den hangs prominently in my study. There is a story behind that painting that God used to indelibly imprint a crucial biblical truth in my heart—a truth that has kept me on the course of faith through many years and numerous trials.

Several years ago an elderly member of our congregation asked me to visit her. We chatted for a while before she drew my attention to the painting of Daniel on her apartment wall. She knew I was enduring some particularly stressful circumstances at the time, and she gave some godly counsel I will never forget.

"Tell me what you see in the painting," she quizzed.

I responded in a matter-of-fact manner. "Well, I see some lions, a few shafts of light, and Daniel."

"There is something else I think you should notice," she continued, obviously aware I had not gotten the message. "Take a closer look at Daniel and you will see that his eyes are not on the lions but on God."

The Holy Spirit instantly gripped me with a spiritual principle that has sustained me in many adversities: When I choose to put my eyes on the Lord, not my situation, God will take me through the problem.

"Looking to Jesus" is not a spiritual cliché. It is a bedrock act of faith anchored to the Scriptures and a spiritual exercise that can mean the difference between victory and defeat in our personal spiritual lives. It is a matter of focus and choice. I can decide whether I will be obsessed with my problems, constantly churning them up in my mind and spirit, or deliberately concentrate on the Lord Jesus Christ, who can help me solve my problems. Dwelling on my circumstances generates anxiety, stress, anger, and fear. It drains me of spiritual vitality and saps

my faith. But choosing to fix my mind on Christ—on his presence and power—builds my faith and provides the right atmosphere for true peace to prevail.

The Greek word the writer of Hebrews used for "fix" literally means to "look away from all else that distracts." I have plenty of distractions each day and so do you. The way to peace is focusing on Christ, feeding on a regular diet of his Word, setting our will to obey his Word, and thanking him that he will fulfill his promises to us.

Are you so overwhelmed that you have lost sight of Jesus? Daniel kept his eyes on heaven, and his troubles on earth were dealt with by the mighty power of God. Fix your gaze on the certainty of God's supernatural help and love, and your problems will be put into perspective. The lion's roar will be stilled.

Father, I am quickly and easily distracted by daily demands. I have so much to do and think about that I lose sight of your presence and goodness. Right now, I choose by faith to look to you for help and guidance. And I trust you for the outcome. Thank you for the peace that you give me as I fix my eyes on you and see the light of your countenance.

TOUCHSTONE

Fix your eyes on Christ, and your problem will be put into perspective.

Now I want you to know, brothers, that what has happened to me has really served to advance the gospel.

Philippians 1:12

Through the Forest

I love the wilderness. I thoroughly enjoy fishing and hunting and the abundant opportunities for scenic photography. The serene surroundings give me plenty of time to contemplate on the greatness and goodness of God. Often the only means by which I can reach many areas is by traversing roughly cut logging roads. The journey is arduous; but the destination is worth the discomfort.

Similarly, hardship is frequently the road we must travel to experience personal peace. That may appear illogical on the surface; but the Bible is filled with examples of men and women facing dire circumstances that paradoxically served to promote, not destroy, God's peace.

The book of Philippians, authored by Paul, is one of the most encouraging epistles in the New Testament. It is upbeat, rings with joy, and has much to say about the peace of God. What is unusual is that Philippians (as well as several of Paul's other letters) was penned from inside a Roman prison, where chains were part of his daily wardrobe. That's not the setting you or I would have in mind for such a joyous epistle, but Paul understood a life-changing principle that can make peace possible in any environment.

He knew that every occasion was an opportunity to "advance the gospel." He seized on a word picture that portrays woodcutters hacking and clearing a trail through forests and hills for armies to tread. Rather than becoming discouraged and faint-hearted, Paul actually saw his problems as divine woodcutters, making a way for the gospel to spread. Is this how you view your obstacles? Can you say with Paul that your circumstances are helping pave the way for Christ to live through you and make himself known to others in the process? You may have some chains of your own—emotional hurts, physical afflic-

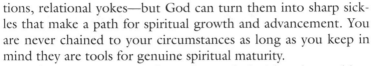

tions, relational yokes—but God can turn them into sharp sickles that make a path for spiritual growth and advancement. You are never chained to your circumstances as long as you keep in mind they are tools for genuine spiritual maturity.

The circumstances and people you deal with today are blazing a trail for the gospel of Christ to become real in your life and a solid testimony to others. It is a rough road, but the view later on can be spectacular.

Thank you, Lord, for the many chances to advance the good news in my life and in the lives of others. I would not choose such sharp tools as you do, but I realize this often is the only way for me to grow and experience your peace. Help me to keep my mind on the result and what is being accomplished as I go through rough times. These difficulties are for my good. They will enhance my communion with you. They will bring about positive results. Never let me lose sight of this truth.

TOUCHSTONE

My circumstances are opportunities to advance the gospel.

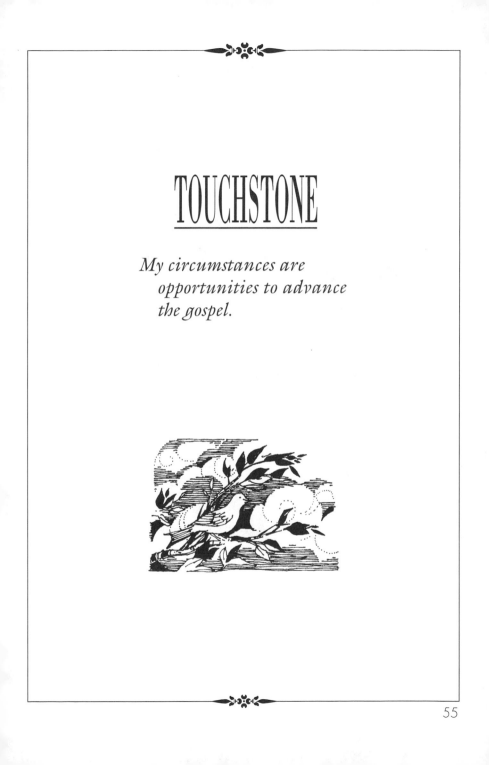

You intended to harm me, but God intended it for good to accomplish what is now being done, the saving of many lives.
Genesis 50:20

Who's in Charge?

A sudden financial crisis can wipe away our carefully con-structed budget. A completely unexpected illness can idle us for months. Unplanned delays can quickly obliterate our carefully crafted schedules.

These scenarios and a multitude of other story lines can leave us with one feeling that can intimidate us more than any other—the feeling that things are out of control. We are usually comfortable with our ability to handle diverse situations. But incidents occur that are beyond the reach of our competence and capability. They shake us to the core. What can we do? How do we handle something that we literally have no control over? How do we experience God's peace in such wildly fright-ening settings?

There is only one prescription for peace in such times—absolute faith in the sovereignty and providence of God. The providence of God has been defined by J. I. Packer as "the unceasing activity of the Creator whereby, in overflowing boun-ty and goodwill, he upholds his creatures in ordered existence, guides and governs all events, circumstances, and free acts of angels and men, and directs everything to its appointed goal, for his own glory." That is not mere theological fluff. That is solid truth you can rely on when your personal world is rocked with calamity, uncertainty, or adversity of any form.

God is in control when all appears out of control. He is able to work good out of evil and to take disastrous events and turn them around for your welfare. As chaotic and happen-stance as some things seem, God is actively working out his benevolent, providential plan for your life. Nothing can thwart his purpose for you. Nothing can shake him.

When you know that God is in control, you can face change—unexpected or anticipated—with confidence. All is held together by his omnipotent hand. All is within his loving care. He is not surprised or frustrated or foiled by anything or anyone. Through God's sovereignty Joseph could see the good hand of God behind his years of enslavement and imprisonment working perpetually to eventually bless him and all of Egypt (Gen. 50:20).

When you know God is in control, you can give thanks in everything, knowing he is arranging all things by his providential care for your personal welfare. It is impossible to be grateful in tough times if you are not resting in the sovereignty of God. When you acknowledge the providence of God, his peace will keep you and guard you. It will steady your soul with the good news that God is in complete control of your circumstances and is working toward his appointed end, which will ultimately benefit you and others.

Thank you that you are a sovereign God. I am not a victim of chance or circumstance but a chosen child of God who belongs to the almighty heavenly Father with whom there is no change. I believe that you are in charge of every area of my life. You are not the author of evil. Evil is only an instrument in your good hand, and nothing can happen to me outside of your permissive will. Thank you for the settling peace this truth brings to me.

TOUCHSTONE

*There is absolutely nothing
that will happen to you
today that your loving
Father doesn't already
know about.*

Grace and peace to you from God our Father and the Lord Jesus Christ.

Galatians 1:3

Grace and Peace

Grace and peace are twin sisters, grace being the firstborn. Where grace abounds, peace thrives. Where grace is stunted, peace shrivels. The salutation of every New Testament letter penned by the apostle Paul contains the hearty greeting "Grace and peace."

If you do not understand grace, you can never understand Christianity. It is a religion of grace. The Bible is the good news of God's grace in Christ Jesus. We begin by grace at salvation and continue by grace each day. We can never earn God's acceptance; we can receive the gift of salvation only through faith in Christ. Once saved, we cannot secure God's approval through good works but only receive the grace of his Spirit to help us accomplish his will.

Grace excludes all human boasting—it boasts only in Christ. It is the perpetual, undeserved goodness and kindness of God that can never be turned away by anything the believer does, says, or thinks. It is the unbroken circle of God's astounding lovingkindness. There is no need to strive for God's love; you already have it through the grace of the Cross. You stand and walk on the same level ground of grace each day.

Think of grace this way: Grace is whatever you may need, whenever you need it. Do you need strength? Grace begets strength. Do you need wisdom? Grace bestows insight. Do you need peace? Grace stills the waters. Do you need comfort? Grace soothes the soul and spirit.

But grace does more than this. Because the fountainhead is God himself, grace gives and gives and gives. The grace of God is not just barely enough to scrape by with. It exceeds and surpasses our most pressing demands. Grace carries you from strength to strength. It gives wisdom liberally. It grants peace that never wanes. It brings comfort that heals and sustains.

You live in the sunshine of God's unconditional grace. You can draw on his inexhaustible, immeasurable, unsearchable reservoir of grace forever and never diminish its fullness. You are no longer under the law, which says "do" and breeds defeat and discouragement, but under grace, which says "done" in Christ and brings triumph and courage.

Paul told Timothy to be "strong in the grace that is in Christ Jesus" (2 Tim. 2:1). When you are "strong in grace," you can stand in any turbulence, face any foe, and deal with any disturbance in the riches of God's complete sufficiency. You are free also to extend grace to others, regardless of their behavior. You swim in the sea of God's grace that buoys you in times of trouble and quenches every thirst. Grace is more than amazing. It's awesome, and it is custom-designed for your every need.

How much I need your grace, O Lord. How quickly I turn to other cisterns of help, all broken and shallow. But when I call on the God of all grace, I receive all I need. I am never disappointed, never short-changed. Thank you for saving me by your grace and keeping me by your grace.

TOUCHSTONE

*Be strong in grace, and
peace will be your
constant companion.*

For from him and through him and to him are all things.

Romans 11:36

The Big Picture

More often than not, it is the little irritations in life that fracture my peace. I usually handle the crises capably, but the accumulation of minor problems can bring great frustration. I don't like to wait in lines. I detest driving in bumper-to-bumper traffic.

Yet I have learned and continue to learn that the petty nuisances of everyday living are precisely God's tools for accomplishing his greatest objective—to conform me to the image of Jesus Christ. That goal was Paul's crown jewel in the cathedral of Romans 8: "For those God foreknew he also predestined to be conformed to the likeness of his Son, that he might be the firstborn among many brothers" (Rom. 8:29).

We actually have the opportunity in this life to be "transformed into his likeness with ever-increasing glory, which comes from the Lord, who is the Spirit" (2 Cor. 3:18). Everything, even the minor irritations, has the potential to be God's instrument for making us like Jesus, to make his will ours, to have his perspective on people and issues.

A visual illustration that helps me understand this principle is my photographic darkroom. When I bring film into the darkroom, the photographic image is already complete. But before it becomes a print, it must go through a harsh developing procedure.

We are complete in Christ. He is in us and we are in him. When we received Christ as Savior, we received his fullness. However, each incident in life, especially the irritations, is a divine developing process that progressively makes us more like him.

What a difference it makes when I keep this big picture in mind. The minor irritations can draw me closer to Christ, making me depend on him in the smallest of details. Because of

this, I can actually give thanks for the irritations. This, of course, as Paul said, comes from the Lord, for I am not capable in my own personality of handling such things with a smile.

What are the little things that annoy you? If you are like me, you have a large list. What happens if you view them as God's tools to allow the life of Christ to be expressed through you? That changes your view doesn't it?

Only in this manner does irritation become inspiration. Like the grain of sand that lodges in an oyster shell and becomes a lovely pearl, the little irritations of life can bring the beauty of Christ's splendor to your inner self.

I don't especially like irritating problems or people, Lord, but I do see the big picture. You have designed everything to help me be like you. That brings meaning to the multitude of aggravations I constantly face. Thank you for the peace this knowledge brings. May Christ's life become mine as I look to him in every detail.

TOUCHSTONE

*Understanding God's big
picture can turn
irritations into
inspirations.*

In all this, Job did not sin by charging God with wrongdoing.
Job 1:22

The Power of Acceptance

When things go wrong, how do you respond? When your prayers are not answered as you envisioned, how do you act? When a problem appears permanent, what is your reaction?

Do you blame others? Do you withdraw? Do you seek an unacceptable behavioral or emotional method of escape? Perhaps we have all tried some of these tactics and discovered their ultimate futility.

The key to knowing God's peace in such instances is acceptance. By acceptance, I do not mean resignation or passivity. I am not talking about developing a martyr complex or nursing self-pity. What I do mean is taking everything as filtered through the benevolent will of God and trusting him for the results, no matter what that may mean.

This is biblical acceptance in the purest sense. Paul questioned God about his thorn in the flesh, even beseeched him to remove it. But God answered, "My grace is sufficient," and Paul came to terms with his weakness. Jesus prayed passionately in the garden before the Cross but obediently submitted his will to the will of the Father. The prophet Habakkuk wondered why God would use the wicked warriors of Babylon as his rod of correction for the Hebrews. Habakkuk's conclusion was that even if the worst happened, he would still rejoice and trust in God (Hab. 3:17–19). Job queried God repeatedly concerning his calamities but ultimately was forced to acknowledge the sovereignty and power of God and his own inability to understand all of God's ways (Job 42:1–6).

Acceptance enables us to deal with life as it really is, not as we dreamed or hoped it would be. It is a crash course in authentic faith, enabling us to put our confidence in God when our questions go unanswered, our problems unresolved, our hopes delayed.

It then enables us to go on, and we can wake up each day with the knowledge that we have put ourselves and our situation squarely in the loving hands of our tender heavenly Father. Nothing may change externally, but we change drastically in our spirit and soul. We can cease depleting our spiritual energy on those things we cannot change by leaving them with God and then work positively toward those things we can change with God's gracious help.

When I fight against my problems, Lord, I have difficulty resting in your peace. I realize now I can accept my conditions, trusting that you are faithfully at work in my life. I will press on to know you, not striving but simply seeking to be fully submitted to you.

TOUCHSTONE

In acceptance there is peace.

For our struggle is not against flesh and blood but against the rulers, against the authorities, against the powers of this dark world and against the spiritual forces of evil in the heavenly realms.

Ephesians 6:12

Dressed for the Battle

The peace of God in the life of the believer does not come cheaply or easily, for we have an adversary, the Devil, who is opposed to our spiritual well-being. We can count on the fact that he is subtly, craftily, and nastily at work to steal our contentment and create confusion and discord. Therefore, we must be alert to his tactics and knowledgeable of our defense against his evil schemes.

Each morning I mentally rehearse the list of spiritual pieces of armor that God provides the believer in Ephesians 6:12–18. I verbally put on each piece as my God-given protection against Satan. I begin with the "belt of truth"—the whole counsel of God, the body of Scriptures—as the foundation for my faith. Satan's primary weapon is the lie. Our most potent weapon is the truth. It defeats him every time. Next, I arm myself with the "breastplate of righteousness." That means I am as holy and acceptable in God's eyes as I will ever be. My sins are forgiven, and Satan has no ground for accusation.

I ready myself with the "gospel of peace." I am an ambassador of God's peace wherever I go. I should be prepared to share Christ, sensitive to the opportunities to bring God's peace to men and women who are alienated from him. Then I purposely take up the "shield of faith," which means I choose to live by faith, not by feelings. I will do what God says regardless of the fickleness of my emotions. Then I put on the "helmet of salvation." That is the challenge to renew my mind according to the truth and the security of knowing I have been delivered from the dominion of sin and Satan into God's kingdom. I am not a slave of sin but a child of God. At that point, I am conscious that I can defeat Satan at every turn with the "sword of the Spirit, which is the word of God." This weapon is particular Scriptures that I can use against the enemy as Jesus did when

Satan tempted him. Find a specific Scripture verse for your situation, memorize it, and use it boldly against the adversary.

You will be amazed at the results when you dress for the battle on a daily basis. Satan's attacks will be foiled, his dark schemes exposed, and his tactics thwarted. Satan was conquered at the Cross by Christ (Col. 2:15), and you can experience the power of his conquest and prevailing peace as you put on the armor designed by God.

Christ Jesus, in you I am a victor over all the power of the enemy. May I learn to put on your triumphant armor each day and enjoy your conquest.

TOUCHSTONE

*Be spiritually well dressed
by putting on the whole
armor of God.*

Come to me, all you who are weary and burdened, and I will give you rest. . . . For my yoke is easy and my burden is light.

Matthew 11:28, 30

Our Burden Bearer

R arely does a day pass when I don't hear the subject of
stress discussed. The topic may be something like
"burnout" or "chronic fatigue." But the real issue is stress, the
pressures of daily life that place us in a weary and parched state
of soul and mind.

J. Hudson Taylor, founder of the China Inland Mission,
understood such pressures. He lived for years in a strange world
with foreign customs. The cultural barriers of sharing the
gospel were great. There was the great burden of administering
a mission agency and the numerous personnel issues that had to
be constantly addressed.

Hanging on the wall of my study is a quote from this godly
man that has helped me personally deal with the stress that is
generated from pastoring a large church and tending to all of
the accompanying duties. It reads: "It doesn't matter, really,
how great the pressure is. It only matters where the pressure
lies. See that it never comes between you and the Lord—then
the greater the pressure, the more it presses you to his breast."

Here is the answer to stress, regardless of its origin, nature,
or intensity: Let the pressure drive you to the Source of all your
strength, peace, and stability—the Person of Jesus Christ. The
apostle Paul came to that wise conclusion after considering the
many hardships he endured: "But this happened, that we might
not rely on ourselves but on God" (2 Cor. 1:9).

Jesus wants to be our burden bearer. He invites us to come
to him with all of our pressures and lay them before him. He
asks us to submit to his lordship and realize that once we are
yoked together with him, he will uphold us. Coming to Jesus in
childlike dependence releases the pressure of our burdens. It
lightens the load and enables us to go on. Instead of crumbling
and fainting, we find new energy, energy that God himself gives

us as we are driven to him.

A method that a friend once shared with me is particularly helpful in laying our burdens down. Lift your hands up to the Lord. In prayer talk to him about your pressures. When you finish, put your hands down. The physical relief is an immediate reminder that you have done business with God and left your burdens with him.

Let your stress press you to Christ. He will never put on you more than you can bear, for he stands with you to shoulder every load. Once you come to Christ and release your burden to him, there is nothing between you and him but sweet peace. His yoke is light and easy and will not pull you down but lift you up in your time of need.

I am so grateful, Father, that you actually invite me to bring my stress points to you. I need relief from these burdens, and that is what you promise as I cast my pressures on you and submit to your clear and peaceful leadership. Thank you for being my burden bearer for sin and the problems of everyday life.

TOUCHSTONE

Give your burdens to Christ.
He has no load limit.

Oh, how I love your law! I meditate on it all day long.
Psalm 119:97

A Threefold Cord

Peace and quiet. They go together, don't they? That is why consistent quiet times alone with God are so indispensable to experiencing the abiding peace of Christ. Yet I must confess that these times of fellowship with the Lord are occasionally dry and uneventful. Out of a desire to see God work more effectively and personally in my life has come a discovery that has enlivened my quiet times and made them more rewarding than ever.

I begin my quiet time with the reading of Scripture. There really is no other way to know God than through the revelation of his Word by the illumination of the Holy Spirit. If Scripture is not the centerpiece of your quiet time, then it will not impart the supernatural life that every word of God contains. After reading (usually one chapter in a book of the Old Testament and another chapter in the New Testament), I pray. God has answered many, many of my prayers. I have come to know Christ intimately. Yet I thirst for something more—something deeper.

I have come to realize that my thirst is quenched as I spend time meditating on the Word of God. Meditation is not mystical. Rather, it is the extremely practical and nourishing exercise of pondering and thinking on what God is saying through his Word. It is the art of asking questions of the Scriptures and then of yourself and discovering how the truth examined can be applied to your life and the particular problems you face.

Until I gave my quiet time the added dimension of meditation, I never received its rich fullness. Here is how I spend such seasons with the Lord. First, I read the Scriptures. Then I meditate on those portions or verses that God seems to highlight as I read. I may turn and look at other Scriptures that address the same subject. But chiefly, I think carefully and soberly about

what the passage says about God and about my response. This takes time. But it is the best investment of time I know.

Then, after reading and meditating on the Scriptures, I turn to the Lord in prayer. I am amazed at how much I have to pray about. My time of meditation is like a greenhouse for prayer. Prayer becomes a sweet release. It is purposeful and directly connected to what God is saying to me through his Word.

If I read but don't meditate, my prayer life is shallow. If I read and meditate but don't pray, I don't have the pleasure of talking with my Savior and the joy of seeing my specific requests answered. Read. Meditate. Pray. This is the threefold cord that will make your quiet times with Christ more productive and powerful than you can imagine. And the peace of God that comes from personal encounters with him will abound.

Lord, help me to be still and know that you are God. Settle me down so that when I read your Word, I can spend time poring over its rich meaning, meditating on its truth, and seeking to apply it to my circumstances. I trust that my quiet times with you will become even more special and bring me great peace.

TOUCHSTONE

*Meditate on God's Word
regularly. It is still waters
and green pastures to
your soul.*

Blessed are the peacemakers, for they will be called the sons of God.

Matthew 5:9

The Hard Work of Peace

K eeping the peace is hard work.
    That is why Paul told the Romans to "make every effort to do what leads to peace" (Rom. 14:19). That is why the author of Hebrews said we ought to "make every effort to live in peace with all men" (Heb. 12:14).

God knows that maintaining relational peace with others is not possible without the diligent, conscious exertion of our will and the restraining of our emotions. At no time, however, are we more like Christ than when we are ambassadors of peace, for it is the peacemakers who are called the "sons of God."

A peacemaker is one who is first concerned about pleasing God, not men. When your motivation is to please men, you are caught in relational snarls that can be almost impossible to untie. Your actions are dictated by circumstances and the personalities of individuals. That is an emotional roller coaster where peace is seldom maintained. But when your desire is always to please God, peace with others is far more likely because then your desire is to do what is right in God's sight, even if the consequences are not pleasant for you.

A peacemaker is also one who cultivates a servant's heart. A servant of Jesus Christ is one who not only acknowledges Christ as Lord but also relinquishes to Christ his personal rights. He is keenly interested in the welfare of other believers and will do what is necessary to promote harmony. That may include some difficult moments of self-denial, such as refusing to voice his opinion or declining to defend himself.

A peacemaker is also one who recognizes the danger of a judgmental or critical spirit and commits himself to the edifica-

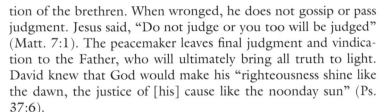

tion of the brethren. When wronged, he does not gossip or pass judgment. Jesus said, "Do not judge or you too will be judged" (Matt. 7:1). The peacemaker leaves final judgment and vindication to the Father, who will ultimately bring all truth to light. David knew that God would make his "righteousness shine like the dawn, the justice of [his] cause like the noonday sun" (Ps. 37:6).

Trusting all judgment to Christ without vested self-interest and consumed with the heart of a willing, humble servant, the believer in Christ is free to become a blessed peacemaker in a world of conflict and hostility. He has entrusted his reputation and reward to Christ himself and becomes his ambassador of reconciliation.

> *It is very difficult, Father, to be a peacemaker. I want to defend myself when conflict arises. Help me to see that you never defended yourself. You did not need to because you were absolutely sure of who you were. I am secure in you. You are the defense of my life. I can bring your peace to others as I confidently rest in my new identity as a new creature in Christ. Make me a peacemaker in my home, my office, my church, wherever I go. I thank you for the blessings you will bring.*

TOUCHSTONE

*If you desire peace,
do the things that make
for peace.*

*No discipline seems pleasant at the time, but painful. Later on,
however, it produces a harvest of righteousness and peace.*
Hebrews 12:11

A Harvest of Peace

The most important truth I have learned as a Christian is that Christ is my life. I am an exhibition of his power, an expression of his grace, and an extension of his life.

However, I did not learn that lesson sitting in my study one day. It lodged in my soul during a very difficult time in my life. After many years of ministry, I reached a point of exhaustion. I was not tired of serving God—I was just tired. I lay in bed for about a week and had to rest physically for several months after that. I could not preach. I could not visit the sick. I could not do any of the things I had been accustomed to doing during my ministry.

It was a painful time, but it was the only way God could get my attention for the most magnificent truth I could learn concerning the Christian life—Christ lives in me so that he may live his life through me. At salvation a great exchange took place—my sin for his righteousness, my sin nature for his holy nature. Since that discovery, my preaching, teaching, and daily living have all been founded on the truth that Christ is my life and that he is sufficient for any task.

You may be passing through a rough season right now. Your finances may be low. Your marriage may be strained. There could be any number of circumstances that could be perplexing you. I want you to consider this possibility: Is your current condition the result of God's disciplining hand? God's discipline is not punishment. It is not judgment. It is not an outpouring of his anger. All of that was put on his Son at Calvary. Rather, his discipline is an expression of his love. It is the love of the heavenly Father who seeks to correct and edify us, not condemn us. God's discipline should actually encourage us because it reminds us that we are his beloved children who matter to him so much that he engages in personal correction.

It was the loving discipline of God that put me out of commission for several months so that I could learn the most important lesson of my life, and I am eternally grateful for that. God knows precisely how to get your attention as well for corrective purposes in your life, and that usually involves unpleasant or uncomfortable conditions.

However, notice that the end result of God's discipline is a "harvest of peace and righteousness." Once corrected, we have exciting new fellowship with Christ that is characterized by a wellspring of peace. Obedience is a delight, not a duty. God's ways are not our ways; but when he disciplines us, it is always in love and for our spiritual benefit. Ask God what he is trying to teach you. Accept his correction, learn his truth, and the truth will set you free.

Lord, I realize that I do not especially like discipline. But when you correct me, you always have a goal in mind—that I may share in your holiness and partake yet more of your divine nature that you gave me at salvation. Help me to discern the times when it is your corrective hand at work and let me quickly learn the liberating truth you yearn for me to know.

TOUCHSTONE

The vinedresser prunes only
for a fruitful harvest.

I can do everything through him who gives me strength.
Philippians 4:13

Peace Through Strength

I was about forty years old at the time. Miss Bertha Smith was more than seventy years old. Meeting her at the airport one evening, I was amazed at her vitality and enthusiasm.

"Miss Bertha," I asked, "why do you always seem to be three steps ahead of me?" I will never forget the reply of this great missionary: "I don't go in my own strength, Charles. I go in the strength of the Lord. If I had been going in my strength, I would have come home from China years ago."

Miss Bertha certainly knew what she was talking about. Although she lived to be ninety-nine years old, the strength she described wasn't physical but spiritual. It was the same type of supernatural energy Paul referred to in his letter to the Philippian church (Phil. 4:13). Was this some sort of idle boast? Was Paul overstating the case? No, he was simply saying that God would enable him to do whatever he had called him to do. That principle has not changed. When we are weak, he is strong. When we are distraught, he is perfectly calm.

God's strength and the peace that follows in its steps begin when we realize our position in Christ. We are "in Christ," a place where the all-sufficiency of the Savior is completely accessible. God is not distant but resident within. All that he is and has is ours because of our personal relationship with him and the presence of the Holy Spirit. "Through him" we can do all things he calls us to do.

It continues with the right perspective on Christ. He is the Creator, Sustainer, and End of all things. He is the Alpha and the Omega. All power and authority is in Christ. Nothing can withstand his might. This is the Christ who lives in us. We must

never diminish the truth that the fullness of deity lives in Christ and we have been given his fullness (Col. 2:9). We do not have to deal with daily problems in human energy but in the resurrection power of Christ.

The question is: Do we tap into this divine fountainhead of God's awesome strength that transforms doubt to confidence, weariness to vigor, and the pessimistic "I can't" to the bold "I can"?

Again, I learned the simple answer from Miss Bertha. She explained, "When I feel burdened and spent, I just pause and remind him of what he promised me and that I am, at this moment, drawing from his resource exactly what I need."

Miss Bertha, Paul, you, and I draw in the same way—by faith. We lean on the promises of God and expect him to do what he says he will do. "Lord Jesus," we say, "I am trusting you for your energy. And I now thank you for it."

In this manner, you can go from strength to strength and find peace that never fails.

> *I do need to go in your strength, heavenly Father. I am so glad that you give me your strength. I do not have to beg or plead for it but receive it by faith. I give thanks for your strength that sustains me and praise you for empowering me whenever I call on your name.*

TOUCHSTONE

God is waiting for you this
very moment to call due
and payable the promises
he has made.

He does not treat us as our sins deserve or repay us according to our iniquities.

Psalm 103:10

Don't Look Back

A former mediocre baseball player raised his batting average almost one hundred points more than the prior season and was named Most Valuable Player in the National League. Asked to explain his dramatic improvement, he said he had learned to focus on the moment at hand. "I don't think about my past at-bats any more," he explained. "I put my failures behind me and concentrate on the present."

Past failures and sins often become the parasitic thief that robs many Christians of God's peace and joy. Somehow such Christians never quite step into the abundant life God has planned for them. They always seem on the verge of stepping into it but are apparently unable to conquer the plague of past mistakes.

The Scriptures are clear on this point: the believer in Jesus Christ is not a victim of his past. He is more than a conqueror through Christ and has the capacity to enjoy each day to its fullest and reach the maximum of his potential for God's kingdom work.

The answer is to understand, embrace, and appropriate by faith each day the radical cure of the Cross—complete forgiveness of sin through Christ's sacrificial death. When Christ died, the guilt and penalty of your sin was placed on him. When you receive him as Savior, you do not have to fear death anymore because Christ died for you. But here is the other part of the good news: You do not have to stagnate in the polluted pool of guilt either, for Jesus was your guilt offering. You can now "draw near to God with a sincere heart in full assurance of faith, having [your] hearts sprinkled to cleanse [you] from a guilty conscience" (Heb. 10:22). God does not condemn you anymore. Why should you condemn yourself? Yes, there may be consequences to your sin that you must still endure, but your

guilt has been taken away. The love and favor of God will help you successfully deal with the aftershocks of sin.

The psalmist said that God has taken away your sin as far as east is from west (Ps. 103:12). That was David's graphic description of God's forgiveness, and he certainly knew the pain of past failures. But his even greater awareness of God's total pardon kept him from belaboring his past defeats and allowed him to become a man after God's own heart.

Is the past stealing today's peace in your life? It doesn't have to anymore. Christ offers you free, full forgiveness so that you may walk in the beauty of his love today and every day. Humble yourself, confess any sin the Holy Spirit convicts you of, receive your pardon in Christ, and concentrate on today's opportunities. You can rise from spiritual mediocrity to a new level of sustained joy and peace in the Lord.

> *Lord, I see now that what I did wrong ten years ago, ten days ago, or ten minutes ago has already been forgiven through Christ's death on the cross. What freedom there is knowing that I am totally forgiven! There is nothing to match it. Teach me to hate sin as you do so that I may understand the incredible depth of your forgiveness. Thank you for removing the chains of guilt and freeing me to face today's challenges with fresh confidence.*

TOUCHSTONE

*You cannot move forward
looking in the rear-view
mirror.*

May the God of hope fill you with all joy and peace as you trust in him, so that you may overflow with hope by the power of the Holy Spirit.

Romans 15:13

Regaining Hope

W hen you have hope for tomorrow, you have the power and peace you need to encounter today's unique set of problems and opportunities. The person who loses hope loses confidence for today and vision for tomorrow. Biblical hope is not fond wishing, it is firm assurance of supernatural help.

Have you reached the point where you are close to giving up hope? Are you so discouraged that the black fog of hopelessness has settled on your soul? That is exactly the place the prophet Jeremiah had reached as he contemplated the destruction of Jerusalem and the temple by the Babylonians.

At the peak of his misery, he inserted this divine ray of hope every believer can cling to in times of despair: "Yet this I call to mind and therefore I have hope: Because of God's great love we are not consumed, for his compassions never fail. They are new every morning; great is your faithfulness. . . . The LORD is good to those whose hope is in him, to the one who seeks him" (Lam. 3:21–23, 25).

When all seems hopeless, hope can be restored as we think about God. It is hard to think about God when our emotions are raw and our confidence is running on vapors, but it is the first step to regaining hope. Deliberately turning your thoughts to God primes the recovery process for hope.

Jeremiah remembered God's great love and compassion. The Hebrew word used for love speaks of the loyal, steadfast, covenant love that God had for his people. God never abandoned them despite sending them seasons of stern discipline. It is that kind of unceasing love that God has for you as his child. It never wanes, it never fails, it never falters. It is not a stale love that lives on past experiences but a daily, renewing, refreshing love that sweeps over your soul moment by moment, day by day. His love is the promise of his provision. Therefore you can

have hope. The love of God for you means that God is now on your side and will stop at nothing to restore your hope in him.

Next, Jeremiah revives his sagging spirit by pondering God's faithfulness. God is faithful to his Word. He will finish what he starts. He is completely trustworthy in every situation and for every unexpected turn of events. Jeremiah also meditates on the goodness of God and the blessings that come from waiting expectantly for him.

The covenant love of God. The unchanging faithfulness of God. The fantastic goodness of God. Think on these things and hope will bear wings that can carry you through every desperate need.

I do lose hope sometimes, Lord. But thank you that you never give up on me. Your love, faithfulness, and goodness are sufficient. I can have hope. I don't have to quit in despair. You are able to uphold me with your strong hand and breathe into me all the hope I need for every load I bear.

TOUCHSTONE

Hope in God is the staircase
out of despair.

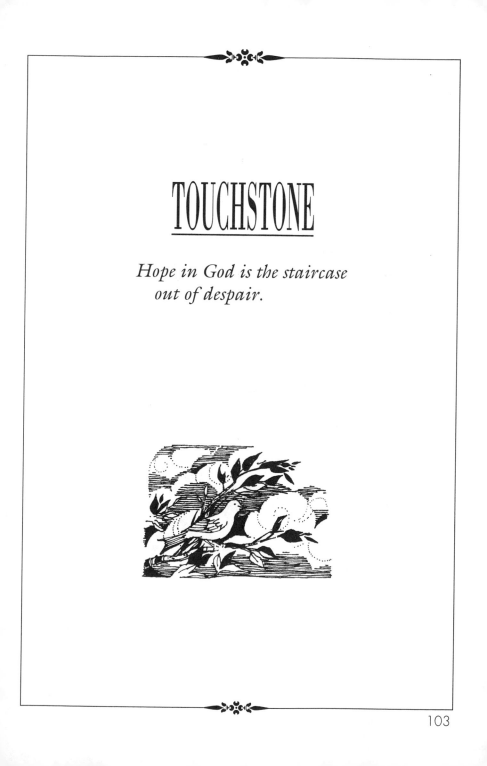

Cast all your anxiety on him because he cares for you.

1 Peter 5:7

Don't Worry, Be Prayerful

When your automobile comes to a stop sign, the intent of the law is for you to come to a complete halt. Disobeying this injunction can result in disaster for you and others.

It was this kind of authoritative force that Paul used when he told the Philippian believers and us, "Do not be anxious about anything . . ." (Phil. 4:6). The original Greek statement is in the imperative tense, calling for the abrupt stoppage of an action. The rich fullness of the Greek can be read in this way: Stop perpetually worrying about even one very little thing. What an amazing command! God is actually forbidding us to worry or fret about anything. Of course, there are normal concerns, but that is not what the Bible is talking about. It is addressing the distracting, anxious cares that gnaw at our soul, allowing little or no room for God's peace to abide. "Just stop it and don't do it anymore," Paul commands.

Easy to say, hard to do. Right? Well, the doing of it is both hard and easy. Hard in the sense that God's Word often asks us to behave in ways contrary to our natural conduct. But it is also easy once we understand that God never asks us to do something for which he does not enable and equip us. Paul's divine prescription against worry is found in the remainder of Philippians 4:6: ". . . but in everything, by prayer and petition, with thanksgiving, present your requests to God."

Paul says in essence that we should worry about nothing by praying about everything. Paul is not referring to a lethargic, generic kind of praying but vigorous, concentrated prayer of the highest sort. The word for prayer suggests the thought and activity of worship and devotion. It is coming to God and rec-

ognizing his power, wisdom, and presence. It is the kind of praying that basks in the greatness of God, exalting his ability to handle all of our worries in his sovereign wisdom.

The use of the word *petition* refers to our specific requests. This is a critical step if we are to truly experience freedom from worry. We first worship God and then present to him our very detailed situation that is causing us to fret. In effect, we are transferring our worrisome circumstance into the capable hands of Almighty God. We are plain, blunt, and to the point in our requests. We don't mince words. We tell God what is bothering us. Then we move into thanksgiving, grateful that our awesome God has heard our requests and will answer us according to his goodness and graciousness. We need not worry. God himself takes on our problems, and his peace replaces our apprehension. Worry is nothing but unbelief. Trusting God with our anxieties through reverent and definitive prayer is the way to stop worry in its destructive tracks and move through our day with the serenity that only God can give.

When I worry, I find it hard to pray. I realize now that prayer is exactly what I need to do in such times. Help me not to wander when I pray but to bring the very thing that troubles me to your attention. Then help me to trust in your ability to handle my worries.

TOUCHSTONE

*Worry about nothing by
praying about everything.*

So David and his men wept aloud until they had no strength left to weep. . . . But David found strength in the LORD his God.
1 Samuel 30:4, 6

From Pity Party to Praise

A pity party is nothing to celebrate, but we have to admit we all have our share of them. They are unproductive, self-defeating, and faith-deflating; and they create a spiritual atmosphere that numbs us to the peace of God.

When David and his warriors returned to their home in Ziklag, they discovered it ravaged and burned. Its inhabitants, including David's family, had been taken captive by the invading Amalekite army. The time was never more ripe for a grand pity party for the former shepherd boy. David's leadership was in question. He had been on the run from Saul for years and fled for shelter among the Philistines, Israel's traditional enemy. David's own soldiers were primed for mutiny and talked of stoning him. David wept. David mourned. David cried. But he turned his pity party around by finding "strength in the Lord his God." While there are no Scriptures that tell how David escaped the suffocating coils of self-pity, I think he must have thought on several things.

I believe David must have reviewed his past. He thought about how God had worked in his life, keeping him from the many schemes and traps of Saul. David probably reflected upon the Lord, considering the intimacy of his personal relationship with Jehovah God and God's faithfulness through the years. Then I imagine that David must have remembered the promises of the God who had taken him from the sheepfold and declared his intent to establish David as king of Israel.

I think David then found strength to go to God in prayer, making a request for God's guidance. We know that David "inquired of the Lord" (1 Sam. 30:8) regarding the pursuit of

the raiding party and found God's specific direction. David gave chase, discovered the camp of the enemy, defeated them, and recovered his family and goods.

What God did for David he will do for you. You do not have to wallow in the mire of self-pity any longer. You can choose to allow God to pull you out of the pit as you review God's past blessings, reflect on the majesty and might of God, remember the promises of God that apply to your particular situation (if you are fearful, find verses on fear; if you feel depressed, search out verses on God's comfort and presence), and then make big requests of God for future guidance and protection.

The pity party will end. Praise will magnify the presence and power of God. You will find victory where there has been defeat, and perfect peace where there has been agony of soul. The choice is yours.

Forgive me for feeling sorry for myself, Lord. That is a dead-end street. Change my perspective so that I may sense your presence and care. Lift me out of the pit and put a new song in my mouth, a song of praise to you.

TOUCHSTONE

When you are in the pit,
God is at his pinnacle.

I have learned the secret of being content in any and every situation.

Philippians 4:12

The Key
to Contentment

One of my favorite spiritual disciplines is reading a chapter of Proverbs each day. A particular passage that has consistently helped me maintain a spiritual equilibrium of contentment and peace is Proverbs 30:8–9: "Give me neither poverty nor riches, but give me only my daily bread. Otherwise, I may have too much and disown you and say, 'Who is the LORD?' Or I may become poor and steal, and so dishonor the name of my God."

Like many, I struggle with the issue of contentment. How much is enough? Should I be satisfied with what I have or seek more? Is ambition wrong? What kind of goals should I have? The answers are not easy, but I believe God's Word provides the balance we need to cultivate godly contentment in our spiritual development and physical needs.

I need to begin with the basics. The most important is a vital, growing relationship with Jesus Christ. That is the foundation for contentment. Only when my chief delight is in Jesus Christ am I able to put into perspective the peripheral issues of material goods and personal ambition. Paul wrote to Timothy, "Godliness with contentment is great gain. For we brought nothing into the world, and we can take nothing out of it. But if we have food and clothing, we will be content with that" (1 Tim. 6:6–8). Concentrate on knowing God and realize that material objects are important only so far as your stewardship is concerned.

That happens as we refuse to be conformed to "the pattern of this world" and become "transformed by the renewing of [our] mind" (Rom. 12:2). The lust of the eyes and the lust of the flesh always want more. They are fast tracks for the allure of deceit and manipulation of a world system riddled with greed and craving. Renewing our mind means we program them with the principles of Scripture. We make decisions based on the truth of God's Word. That keeps us on an even keel when the pull of the world tugs disproportionately at our pocketbooks or hearts.

We must learn to live on a daily basis. Jesus told us to pray for our "daily bread"—the sufficient provision for today's necessities. Contentment most often is lost when we worry about the future. God is in control of that, and we must leave tomorrow's problems with him. Today I can bring my needs to Christ. Today his grace is sufficient. Jesus "daily bears our burdens" (Ps. 68:19).

Above all, the key to contentment is learning that I can do everything God wants me to do through his enablement. I can set faith-building goals that are in God's will. Ambition is okay so long as my chief objective is to glorify Christ, not myself. God does not want us to do everything, but he will help us do what he has planned for our lives. We can be content knowing that he empowers us to deal with all the ups and downs of life as we wholeheartedly depend on him.

Contentment is a daily battle. It is something we learn by sticking to the basics—nurturing a growing relationship with Jesus Christ, living one day at a time, and knowing that Christ in us strengthens us for every challenge. This is great gain and gives great peace.

Contentment is hard to learn. But I know, Lord, that you can give me peace in every circumstance and the contentment it brings as I submit to your lordship. Teach me to trust you for each day's problems and rely on you to strengthen me for every task. I can be content as long as I know you are with me, helping me at every turn.

TOUCHSTONE

*A contented heart is one
that allows Christ to set
the agenda.*

See to it that no one misses the grace of God and that no bitter root grows up to cause trouble and defile many.

Hebrews 12:15

Rooting Out Bitterness

One of the greatest barriers that prevents us from experiencing God's unsurpassed peace is a root of bitterness. Planted as a seed of anger, rejection, or resentment, bitterness grows into a poisonous emotion that chokes out the peace of God in our lives and defiles the lives of family members and friends.

If you are or have been embittered against someone because of an unjust circumstance, you know the emotional price you pay. It affects you physically and spiritually, releasing its hostile toxins at the slightest upset. You cannot hide a bitter spirit. It spills over into all that you do.

But the good news of the gospel is freedom from every form of bondage, including a bitter spirit. You do not have to be its slave or allow it to fester a day longer. In honest prayer before God, admit your bitterness. Be specific. Acknowledge it as sin and repent, changing your mind and heart about its corrosive influence. This attacks the problem at its root—sin against God—and creates the right climate for healing and restoration.

Next comes one of the most difficult steps toward dislodging the stronghold of bitterness. You must choose to view the offending party or circumstance as God's tool in your life. That is fundamental to long-term freedom. Everything that comes into your life is filtered through the will of God. God has allowed this person or event, as painful as it may be, to touch your life for your personal spiritual growth. This is the extraordinary biblical view that will excavate the root of bitterness from your spirit. You are not a victim of injustice or vengeance

but a child of God who can respond to every circumstance in the light of the fact that he is in control and he has allowed it for his good purpose.

Accepting that truth allows you to move on to extending grace and forgiveness. You did not deserve God's grace. Others do not deserve his grace. But he freely extends it to you regardless of your performance. You are called to freely extend it to others who hurt you as well. There is no limit to forgiveness or grace. When you forgive another person, choosing to treat others as Christ treats you, then you are replacing the cancer of bitterness with the superabundant, healing love of God. "Be kind and compassionate to one another, forgiving each other, just as in Christ God forgave you" (Eph. 4:32).

Bitterness causes us to come short of God's grace, not to fall from it. Let the grace of God do its work in your heart, and bitterness will have no room to sprout and spread.

Dear Lord, when you hung on the cross, you had no bitterness toward your persecutors because you knew they were tools in your Father's hand to accomplish the marvelous work of redemption through your death, burial, and resurrection. May I see those who offend me in this same divine light and so be rescued and delivered from the venom of a bitter spirit. Thank you for your grace and forgiveness that make healing possible.

TOUCHSTONE

*Bitterness can find no root
in the rich soil of grace.*

Be transformed by the renewing of your mind. Then you will be able to test and approve what God's will is—his good, pleasing and perfect will.

Romans 12:2

Peace and Good Will

When I came to First Baptist Church of Atlanta more than twenty years ago, I encountered much opposition. One truth sustained and kept me through the many conflicts: I knew I had obeyed the will of God. He had put me there. I could accept the challenges with complete confidence.

There is little peace for the person who consistently follows his own instincts instead of seeking God's plan. But the person who knows he is in step with Christ can experience steady peace even in tight places. When Paul and Silas were called by God to preach in Macedonia, they quickly found themselves in a prison cell. But they sang praises instead of grumbling, because they knew they had followed God obediently and wholeheartedly.

"But if God would just send angels and tell me where to go and what to do, I could sing praise psalms as well," you say. I understand. I feel that way sometimes too. But what I have realized is that God has given me the full revelation of his Word to impart wisdom and counsel sufficient for every demand. He has not left me to grope in the dark. The light of his Word is available for my decision making, and the Holy Spirit lives in me to make it clear.

The key is to be principle-centered. A Bible principle is an eternal truth with universal application. For instance, we reap what we sow. If you hang around bad friends, trouble is not far away. God may not tell me which house to buy or which car to drive, but his principles of finance provide accurate guidelines. If you stay in the Scriptures, your desire to do God's will eventually intersects with a principle of Scripture. We must do more than pull Bible promises out of the scriptural hat, accept them as God's confirmation, and move on.

Sometimes God will use a certain verse to direct us; but most often, he leads us by aligning our decisions with biblical principles. We must be willing to seek God's will. He invites us to ask him for guidance and wisdom because he cares for us. He wants us to do his will because he desires that we glorify him. It is not that we have to overcome God's hesitance to impart information; we have only to receive humbly and patiently what he gladly gives. Even when we make the wrong decision and reap the unpleasant consequences, we are never outside the love of God. We admit our mistake, confess our sin if we were disobedient, and then trust God to lead us from that point.

We must keep in mind that God is most interested in revealing himself in the decision-making process. He wants us to know him as the Guide rather than merely receiving right guidance from him. He wants to us know him supremely.

You can know and do the will of God. It is not complex. Live in obedience to him, read and study his Word, wait for his answer, and more than likely you will find yourself doing the good, pleasing, and perfect will of God. In his will is a stable, fixed peace.

Lord, it is good to know that you desire for me to know your will even more than I desire to know it. I am your servant; and like any servant, I receive my directions from the Master. I understand that it may take time for your will to be grasped, but I thank you for giving me enough truth and light to make daily decisions that move me in your direction. Above all, thank you for drawing me closer to you. And the better I know you, the more likely I will discover your plan.

TOUCHSTONE

*Seek the Guide, and
guidance is sure
to follow.*

And the peace of God, which transcends all understanding,
will guard your hearts and your minds in Christ Jesus.

Philippians 4:7

Peace of Mind

Peace of mind. Everyone is looking for it. Only God can deliver it. It is a peace detached from external factors, above and beyond sheer logic, victorious over raw emotions.

It is the kind of peace every follower of Christ can access. It is not reserved for merely tragic moments, though it certainly is sufficient in such instances. It is available in unlimited portions for everyday living, every decision, every obstacle, every circumstance.

There is, of course, no formula for such peace, for it is tailor-made by the God of peace for each individual, for each situation. There are, however, several pervasive principles of Scripture that are spiritual pathways to this exquisite peace of heart and mind.

Peace that passes understanding is grounded on a spiritual mindset: "The mind controlled by the Spirit is life and peace" (Rom. 8:6). The mind controlled by the Spirit views all of life from God's perspective. It is constantly nourished by the Word of God and is focused on the priority of spiritual principles above the philosophy and mindset of the world. It filters all of our thoughts, emotions, and contemplations through the pure grid of the Scriptures. Our minds are yielded to the Spirit's influence and direction.

Such peace is experienced as we avoid the worrisome tug of double-mindedness. James wrote that the double-minded man is "unstable in all he does" (James 1:8). The believer asks God for wisdom, makes his requests clearly known, and then thanks God for the answer. He is singled-minded in that he expects God to act and refuses to entertain the twin evils of doubt and unbelief.

Transcendent peace is cultivated by thinking on the things that Paul calls "true, noble, right, pure, lovely, admirable, excel-

lent, and praiseworthy" (Phil. 4:8). You are called to have your mind dwell on good things and think cheerfully about the future. Positive thinking is simply allowing your mind to meditate on truth. Your mind is renewed. Your personality is reprogrammed by the powerful, living Word of God to think as he thinks.

When all this is done, you can say along with Paul that "the God of peace will be with you" (Phil. 4:9). Peace of mind inevitably leads to peaceful living. A supernatural quality of contentment and calm rests at the center of your heart, protecting and shielding you from the excessive fretfulness of this world. Chaos may swirl around you, but you are anchored to the unchanging peace of Christ.

The Source of peace gives transcendent peace. It is for you. It is for you today. It is a gift you receive by confident faith. Embrace it, and you will not exchange it for anything the world may offer.

Jesus, I am truly amazed how you give your peace for everyday living. When I am torn apart, your peace calms me as I turn aside from the distractions and allow the Holy Spirit to control my thoughts. Sometimes your peace rushes in. Sometimes it takes awhile. But it does come as I continue to gaze upon you. Be the health of my countenance, O Lord, as you guard my emotions and thoughts with your shield of peace.

TOUCHSTONE

*The Source of peace
gives transcendent
peace to you.*

So we say with confidence, "The Lord is my helper; I will not be afraid. What can man do to me?"

Hebrews 13:6

Preparing
for the Future

The most prevalent emotion concerning the future is fear. Since we do not know what tomorrow holds, we lean toward a degree of tension and uncertainty, which breeds timidity and undermines our confidence in God. Of course, certain fears are appropriate. We should be afraid to stick our hands in a snake den or a hot fire. That's only common sense. But there are hordes of unnecessary, unhealthy fears of today and tomorrow that erode our peace and create unsettled spiritual footing for fighting the good fight of faith.

Knowing that God is in control of all things should lessen much of our apprehension. We know that God is with us, so we can obey the many scriptural injunctions that tell us, "Fear not . . ." But often our fears are so stubbornly ingrained that it takes more than a knowledge of God's providence and an awareness of his presence to put fear to flight.

Here is one biblical principle that has helped me deal with my personal fears and I believe will comfort and encourage you too: The more I understand and accept God's amazing love for me, the less I fear life's uncertainties. That was the apostle John's antidote for fear: "There is no fear in love. But perfect love drives out fear. . . . The one who fears is not made perfect in love" (1 John 4:18).

God cares for me with absolutely perfect love. That means he is taking care of all my needs, including my future ones. As I rest in his constant, unceasing love for me, fear is banished. What do I need to be afraid of if God himself is caring for me? Why should the future frighten me if God promises he will provide his all-sufficient love for every situation? Bask in the love of

God. Think on the love of God. Embrace the love of God. When you do, the many concerns and issues that can generate fear will be expelled by the awesome love of God.

If we allow our fear to drive us to a greater appreciation and appropriation of the love of God, then our fears actually lead us to greater trust and dependence on the Father. David said, "When I am afraid, I will trust in you" (Ps. 56:3). God does not give you fear but power, love, and a sound and well-balanced mind (2 Tim. 1:7). As a ship's weight displaces water, the love of God will dislodge all your fears.

Jesus told the crowds, "Do not be afraid, little flock, for your Father has been pleased to give you the kingdom" (Luke 12:32). You are a member of the flock under God's care. He will never leave or forsake you. That truth should melt your fears. It should dissolve your alarm and terror. You are a sheep in God's fold, and God takes perfect care of his flock. The Good Shepherd loves you and provides for you. May every apprehension thaw under the light of God's perfect love for you.

I am not sure I understand how perfect your love for me is, Father, but I do know that it is better than I can possibly imagine. My fears, and I do have several, have no place when I allow your love to govern and guide me. Every trace of terror is gone when I think of being under your watchful care. Thank you for the peace and security that truth brings and help me to apply it daily. When fear arises, may it drive me into your love and so make me more dependent on you and less susceptible to the "what ifs" of life.

TOUCHSTONE

God knows all of your "what ifs" and has provided all of the "will be's" for them.

Your promises have been thoroughly tested, and your servant loves them.

Psalm 119:140

An Encouraging Word

In the margin next to many Scripture verses in my Bible are clearly marked dates. Each one indicates an instance when God spoke to me through the verse to encourage me in times of testing or adversity. I cannot tell you how many times a Bible promise has sustained me in difficult straits. It is light in darkness, strength in weakness, and nourishing manna for my soul.

A Bible promise is God's Word of encouragement for you to claim by faith and cling to in rough waters. When a battered Paul was hesitant to stay in Corinth, God promised him safekeeping (Acts 18:9–10). When the ship that was transferring him to Rome was about to sink, God sent an angel to Paul to declare that he would stand before Caesar and the lives of all those aboard would be spared (Acts 27:23–24). When Joshua prepared to enter the Promised Land, God encouraged him with the assurance of his presence and deliverance from the land's inhabitants (Josh. 1:2–9).

A Bible promise from God is a declaration of his intention to graciously bestow a gift upon his children. Some promises are conditional, fulfilled only upon the believer's obedience to a clearly stated condition. For example, if you want to experience God's best financially, you must first give of your resources. Other promises have specific limitations, such as God's covenant promise to Abraham that he would become the father of many nations. But there are many promises God desires to see claimed and appropriated in our lives that require only trust in him.

God's promises usually meet a specific need in your life. You may be reading the Scriptures, and a verse becomes divinely highlighted by the Holy Spirit. This is a promise from God you may claim if you do not take it out of context (manipulate it to apply to an irrelevant situation) and if your interpretation of it does not contradict any other portion of Scripture. The Spirit of God witnesses to your spirit that it is from him, and the ultimate purpose is to glorify God.

When God speaks to you in such a way, you have a promise that will anchor your mind, will, and emotion. You can meditate on it day and night, standing on the authority and power of the Word of God. It becomes part of your being.

God's promises have never let me down. God cannot lie. If you will discipline yourself to read his Word consistently and obediently and wait patiently and submissively for him to fulfill his promises, you will discover truth you can stand on in any weather. Nothing promotes peace like God's encouraging Word.

Thank you, Lord, for inviting me to stand on your promises. I know I can count on you. When you speak to me in this way, I am greatly blessed. I have the strength to endure, the hope to continue. Make me sensitive to your Word and bold to claim your promises.

TOUCHSTONE

A Bible promise is God's guaranteed means of encouragement.

A Touch of His Love

Contents

Photographs

Acknowledgments

To a highly valued member of our In Touch staff, Jim Daily, I express my deepest appreciation for his helpful editorial assistance for this volume.

And to Tim Olive, my photographer friend with whom I shared the unforgettable experience of shooting and printing these photographs, my sincere thanks.

Introduction

I was headed for burnout, but I didn't know why. I called together four of my friends and asked them to meet and pray with me. Thankfully, they did, and my time with them led me to a fresh discovery of God's love.

From that day on, I began to experience and "feel" God loving me; and it has never been the same. Since that moment, God, whom I had followed and obeyed all my life, became my Friend. I had new intimacy with the Savior; and I soon found that the more I loved him, the more I trusted him.

Knowing, receiving, and extending the love of God is the essence of the Christian faith. There is nothing more powerful, more encouraging, more settling, than embracing the love God has for you. God loves you as much today as he ever will, so you don't have to perform perfectly. He has pledged his unfailing love to you in every circumstance.

A Touch of His Love unveils the power and reality of the love of God. It is my prayer that Christ's unconditional love for you will saturate your mind and spirit and remove any false perceptions you may have about the character and ways of God.

The love of God is the big picture that puts everything else in right perspective. That was Jesus' emphasis when he said that the sum of Christian living is to love God enthusiastically and to love your neighbor as yourself (Matt. 23:37–39). That dispels petty rules and legalistic lifestyles that nullify the amazing grace and love of Christ.

My friend, whatever you face today, remember that Jesus is the same God "yesterday, today, and forever" (Heb. 13:8). That means that wherever you are and whatever you need, God loves you.

That is all you need to know.

A Touch of His Love

We know and rely on the love God has for us.

1 John 4:16

Experiencing God's Love

Something was missing. Somehow, after twenty years of ministry, I sensed I had an incomplete picture of and relationship with my Savior. I still preached every week. I continued to practice essential spiritual disciplines. However, something was definitely amiss in my own soul.

I became so restless and dissatisfied that I called four of my friends, all Christian counselors, and asked them to meet with me. It was on short notice, but amazingly, they all agreed. We sat down together on a Monday afternoon. Until late the next morning, they quizzed me, conversed with me, and endeavored to help me find the answers I was seeking.

I poured my heart out to God and these men, but there was still no release or rest in my spirit. As we were about to conclude, one of them said to me, "Charles, put your head on the table. Imagine that your father just picked you up in his arms. What do you feel?"

An emotional dam burst precisely at that moment. I wept for a long time. In fact, I had a difficult time stopping. I wasn't sure what God was doing, but he had obviously touched the most sensitive spiritual nerve of my soul.

When I settled down, the same person asked me how I felt. "I feel warm and secure and loved," I replied and immediately began weeping again. This time, however, I realized what God was doing.

I had trusted God since I was a small child. I had no trouble obeying him. I understood the importance of prayer and the priority of God's Word. What I never truly embraced or experienced, however, was the love of God. His sweetness and loving-kindness had somehow remained a footnote in my Christian walk. That is why I seldom preached any messages on the love of Christ. How could I preach what I had not personally experienced?

Through the godly help of my friends and the tender ministry of the Holy Spirit, I was able to identify the cause of that inner void. You see, my father died when I was an infant, and I simply didn't understand what the Father love of God was all about.

That encounter radically changed my life. Everything took on new purpose and meaning. My fellowship with God entered a new dimension. It was as if I started the Christian life all over again.

There may be something in your life that hinders you from fully experiencing and enjoying the most marvelous, liberating power in heaven and earth—the superabundant, absolutely transforming love of God. Quiet yourself before God for a season and ask him to make you newly aware of his love for you. Let him use whatever instrument he chooses and work in whatever way he determines.

Like me, you will begin a fantastic new adventure with God that sweeps away the dregs of the past and pours a fresh foundation for a vibrant, personal friendship with Jesus Christ, the lover of your soul.

God, help me to understand anew the vastness of your love. I know intellectually that you love me; but I want to experience it for myself, not simply read about it or examine it in a Bible study. Draw me into your love and keep me there.

TOUCHSTONE

The adventure of God's love never ends.

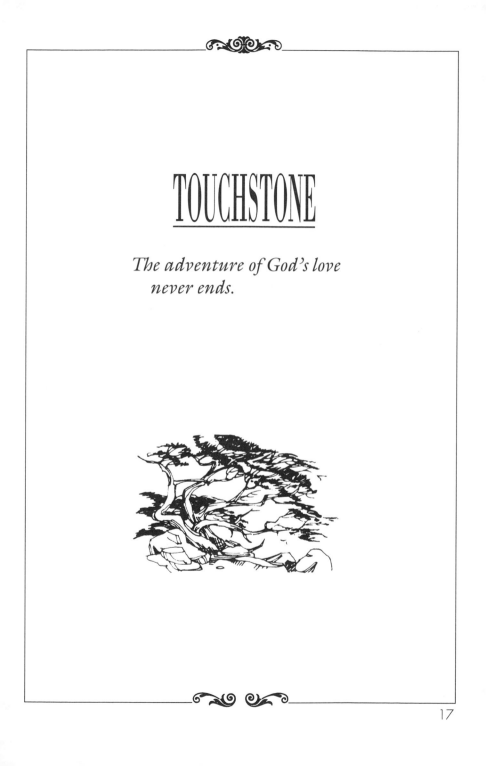

As the Father has loved me, so have I loved you. Now remain in my love.

John 15:9

The Pattern of Love

While other religions of the world present strict and complicated teachings or devise complex philosophies, Christianity shouts that "God is love" (1 John 4:16). What a contrast and what relief!

But that should not surprise us, because throughout eternity, there has been a spectacular love relationship between the Father and his Son. Before the creation of the world and man, before time, Jehovah God and his only begotten Son lived in a perfect love relationship.

Although God loves man lavishly, he first bestows his perfect love on his Son, who in turn loves the Father joyously and unceasingly. And though there is no mention of the Father's love for the Holy Spirit, we know that the Trinity was and is ablaze with pure, unadulterated love, because the Spirit's desire is to glorify the Son.

After Jesus was baptized by John the Baptist, the Father in heaven expressed his delight with the Savior, announcing to all: "This is my Son, whom I love; with him I am well pleased" (Matt. 3:17). Jesus told the Jews that "the Father loves the Son and shows him all he does" (John 5:20). Speaking intimately to his disciples at the Passover Supper, Christ said plainly, "I love the Father . . ." (14:31).

Any attempt to coldly calculate the Trinity or to describe the ministry and relationship of the Father and the Son apart from divine love is not the true gospel; for every biblical principle, every utterance of Scripture is bathed in the love of God and the love of Christ.

Still more amazing is that the kind of love that exists between the Father and the Son can be experienced by you and me. Again teaching his hand-picked disciples at the Passover Feast, Jesus astounded them with these words: "As the Father has loved me, so have I loved you. Now remain in my love" (John 15:9).

The love of God the Father for his Son and the love of the Son for his Father are gladly dispensed to every Christian. God invites you through faith in his Son to share his love. His love has been deposited in your heart. Jesus cares for you with the same kind of love that the Father demonstrated to him. Can you imagine abiding, living, and resting in this incredible love?

Lord, today I especially need to sense your comforting love and protection. My days usher in new challenges at every corner, and it's during these moments that I need to experience your love and comfort. When I ponder the way you comforted your Son, Jesus Christ, as he faced death on a cross, I am strengthened and renewed for each day.

TOUCHSTONE

Jesus cares for you.

*The LORD is close to the brokenhearted and saves those who are
crushed in spirit.*

Psalm 34:18

Of Reeds and Wicks

Have you ever tottered on the edge of despair, so disillusioned and disheartened that you wondered if God really loved you anymore? Have you been so wounded by painful circumstances or another's distressing actions that you questioned if God could really heal your hurt?

We all have experienced the anguish of such moments; and if our perspective on the love of Christ is clouded, we can succumb to spiraling depression and bitterness. How grateful I am that our Savior comes to our aid at such times with tender love.

In describing the nature of the coming Messiah's ministry, the prophet Isaiah said, "He will not shout or cry out, or raise his voice in the streets. A bruised reed he will not break, and a smoldering wick he will not snuff out" (Isa. 42:2–3).

More than eight hundred years later, Matthew thought of Isaiah's words and used them to describe Jesus' earthly life as he healed broken bodies and relieved tormented minds, touching the lives of physically and emotionally damaged people. Some were blind and mute, even demon-possessed. Most, no doubt, were social outcasts. But Jesus, with exquisitely sensitive compassion, changed their dreary, desperate world into one of renewed hope and confidence. And the One who does not change is poised to illumine darkness with the radiant light of his love.

If you feel like a "bruised reed" about to break or a "smoldering wick," your soul exhausted and almost extinguished, take courage. The love of God is both strong and tender enough to heal your hurts and revive your spirit. At your weakest moment, God's love is completely sufficient to sustain you.

You can count on God's tender mercy to rescue and restore you in your darkest hours. The Great Physician quietly comes into your pain and goes about doing what he does best—touching, healing, restoring men and women who are weary. He never snuffs out the slightest plea for hope, the parched cry for relief and help. Just call on him. He's already there, with healing in his wings, eager to impart strength for the journey.

That's good news, isn't it?

Lord, I am hurting right now, to the point of numbness. The only comfort I truly have at this moment is knowing that you are gently holding me in your arms. It makes me realize that you have always been faithful to get me through the storms. This gives me the confidence and comfort to carry on.

TOUCHSTONE

*Jesus' tender love is the
rainbow at the end
of a storm.*

We meditate on your unfailing love.

Psalm 48:9

Unfailing Love

If there is one topic that I delight in meditating upon repeatedly, it is the object of the psalmist's contemplation—the unfailing love of God. Nothing so comforts me, so steadies me, so nourishes me as the truth of God's unfailing love for his people.

The writers of the Old Testament used the rich Hebrew word *hesed* to express this characteristic of God's care. It is sometimes translated "loving-kindness" or "steadfast love." It incorporates the staggering reality that God's love simply cannot let his people go.

Flowing unceasingly from the heart of God is love that will never let you down, never disappoint you, never forsake you, never fail you. The writer of Hebrews said it this way: "Never will I leave you; never will I forsake you" (Heb. 13:5).

The steadfast love of God never changes, is never diminished by my behavior, is never quenched by my indifference or even rebellion. The loyal, covenant-keeping love of Christ is ever fresh, ever healing, ever faithful, ever sufficient.

Since God's love for you is unfailing and unchanging, you need not be unsettled. "For the king trusts in the LORD; through the unfailing love of the Most High he will not be shaken" (Ps. 21:7). Those were the words of David, whose life was constantly in peril. His safety and stability rested securely in God's remarkable love for him, and so do yours.

I would like to suggest a spiritual exercise that I believe can revolutionize your knowledge of God and your relationship with him. The concept is expressed in the oldest psalm of the Bible, penned by Moses: "Satisfy us in the morning with your unfailing love, that we may sing for joy and be glad all our days" (Ps. 90:14).

Each morning, think upon God's unfailing love, how it is expressed to you, its immensity, its power, its nature. Let God satisfy you with the sure knowledge that he has set his love upon you and will never turn it away. The more frequently you ponder God's boundless love, the more joyful you will become. The more joyful you are, the more exciting is your walk with Jesus and the more dynamic is your faith.

The unfailing, steadfast love of Christ for you is your anchor for every storm, sustaining you, keeping you, upholding you. It satisfies the deepest longing of your heart.

Heavenly Father, I can hardly imagine what your unfailing, unceasing love really means. I do know that it is what I yearn for in my heart. Each day, grant me a more complete understanding of how much you really love me. Along the way, teach me how to express that love to those around me. Thank you for creating the need for love within me and supplying that need. Amen.

TOUCHSTONE

*The love of God will never
let you down.*

For great is his love toward us.

Psalm 117:2

Receiving God's Love

One of the first verses of Scripture I learned as a young Christian (and probably the verse most believers can quote from memory) is John 3:16: "For God so loved the world that he gave his one and only Son, that whoever believes in him shall not perish but have eternal life."

As I have grown in Christ, I understand that the entire Bible, every verse, is the revelation of God's love for mankind. From Genesis to Revelation, it is the story of Christ's unflagging desire to redeem and reconcile human beings to an eternal fellowship with himself.

How then did I develop such stubborn resistance to receiving and enjoying God's love? Why are so many other Christians caught in the same spiritual snarl that ties up our fellowship with God and dangerously entangles our whole viewpoint of the Christian life? We know that God is love, but our knowledge of his love runs only skin deep. We know much about sound doctrine, but our soul is starved for the love of God.

There are some basic factors involved. Perhaps the most obvious is pride, the taproot of sin. It is a devilish snare that promotes the deceptive thinking that once God has rescued us from eternal ruin, we can make it on our own. It binds us in an exhausting, exacting lifestyle that rarely displays Christ's character and seldom satisfies us. Pride repels the love of God. It breeds self-reliance, short-   circuiting our need for love.

Yet beyond pride, I feel there is still a rather common malady that kept me and prevents others from even having a clue of what Christ meant when he said, "Now remain in my love" (John 15:9). Jesus used the Greek word *agape*. This word was seldom used by the Greeks and had little cultural weight, but Jesus and the writers of the New Testament injected it with supernatural significance, using it to express the unconditional love of God for the believer.

Unconditional love means this—God loves you just the way you are. Isn't that something we all ache for, to be loved without conditions or stipulations? God loves you when you obey, and he loves you when you err. That doesn't mean he tolerates sin—he died for it—or that he dilutes its consequences. But it does mean that his love for you is amazingly steadfast and unchanging.

Perhaps it is because the concept is so alien that we know embarrassingly little about God's agape love. But that can change today. God loves you as much now as he ever will. God's love is freely bestowed on you by his choice. It may sound too good to be true, but it is God's idea. Receive it, accept it, and you will never be the same.

Heavenly Father, I did not realize that pride can take root so subtly. I am probably unknowingly struggling with its snare. Expose those areas where its roots are cutting off complete devotion to you. As I humble myself, reveal your words of love throughout Scripture so I may be solidly grounded in an understanding of agape love.

TOUCHSTONE

For God so loved me, he gave his Son so I can have eternal life.

We have peace with God through our Lord Jesus Christ, through whom we have gained access by faith into this grace in which we now stand.

Romans 5:1–2

The Cure of Grace

I admit I have a "type-A" personality. I like well-defined goals. I enjoy accomplishment. I want to do things better. There is nothing inherently wrong with this mind-set, but it can lead to a biblically deficient lifestyle that defuses the awesome power of God's grace.

The gospel is the good news of God's grace. Jesus was full of "grace and truth" (John 1:14). The message of the apostles was the triumph of grace over law. Apart from the cornerstone of grace, the gospel would be fundamentally flawed. You cannot understand Christianity or the love of Christ until you major on grace.

Grace is God's kindness and graciousness toward humanity without regard to the worth or merit of those who receive it and in spite of the fact that they don't deserve it. God's grace toward the believer means that we cannot do anything to make God love us any less or any more. Think on that!

What this does (to type-A personalities like me, as well as to every other human disposition) is dismantle the tiresome treadmill of performance. I don't have to be successful to be loved. I don't have to fulfill certain obligations to be loved. I am loved by the God of all grace because there is nothing I can do to earn or merit his love.

What a wreckage this makes of our traditional thinking. But that is precisely what grace does. It goes against our grain because it flows from the fountain of God's supernatural love. We don't have to do anything to merit God's pleasure; we already are pleasing to him once we receive Christ's forgiveness of sin.

If that sounds radical, you're right. Grace says, "You can't—I can." It says, "You've failed. That's okay. I will help you. I will restore you." You can do nothing to earn salvation because it is a gift of God's grace. And you can do nothing to merit his continued favor, for, as Paul says, it is grace "in which we now stand."

Are you working hard to gain God's favor? You have it. Is there always something more you think you have to do in order to be accepted? God has done all you need through the cross of Christ to make you acceptable.

We are saved by grace through faith (Eph. 2:8). We live to the praise of his grace (1:6) and are enjoined to be strong in the grace of God (2 Tim. 2:1). Christ's performance on the cross has been credited to your account so you can be free to live life "to the full" (John 10:10). It is a sufficient promise.

Lord, I've been plagued with feelings of guilt lately, believing I wasn't doing enough to earn your fellowship. But Romans 5 tells me I already have peace with you because of your grace. I don't have to do or be anything! Jesus Christ did it all. I want to spend the next few moments thanking you and meditating on the reality of being totally accepted by you—just as I am.

TOUCHSTONE

*You cannot do anything
today to make God love
you any more or any less.*

This is love: not that we loved God, but that he loved us and sent his Son as an atoning sacrifice for our sins.

1 John 4:10

Supreme Love

Do you ever question God's love for you? Do you sometimes feel as if you have somehow wandered outside the sphere of his compassion into a bewildering state of turmoil and problems?

When such disconcerting thoughts and feelings disturb you—as they do most of us—there is a remedy that can keep you from stumbling into despair and discouragement. The cure for this sentiment is the cross of Jesus Christ. Whatever doubts you may entertain about God's love for you can be instantly dispelled when you consider the anguish and benefits of Christ's crucifixion.

Jesus' brutal death on a Roman cross is the highest expression of God's love for man. Seated in divine royalty in the heavenlies, Jesus was sent to earth by the Father to execute his eternal plan for man's redemption. When you think of Jesus impaled on coarse timbers, hanging, hurting, bleeding, you are pondering the greatest act of love ever displayed.

For it was on the killing field of Golgotha that the sinless One took on our sins, incurring the holy fury of the Father against iniquity so we might inherit the glory of eternal life. Jesus died for you. He suffered for your sin. And wonder of wonders, he did this while mankind was still in rebellion against him. "But God demonstrates his own love for us in this: While we were still sinners, Christ died for us" (Rom. 5:8).

As he always does, God took the initiative to save mankind from sin and death. He made the first move by eliminating the obstacle of unforgiven sin through his all-sufficient, sacrificial, atoning death. Christ on the cross says "I love you" in the most endearing way possible.

Never doubt the love of God for you. Turn your focus on Christ's substitutionary death on your behalf. Think upon what he did for you and what he is willing to do today. For if "he . . . did not spare his own Son, but gave him up for us all—how will he not also, along with him, graciously give us all things?" (Rom. 8:32). The love that sent Jesus to die your death lives in you to provide for every need in every circumstance. It is undying love that will never let you down. That is the truth, the truth that will set you free.

Jesus, thank you for showing your utmost love by dying on a cross for me. When I doubt that you care, refocus my attention on Calvary. It is the eternal proof of your love.

TOUCHSTONE

*The cross is the proof
of God's love.*

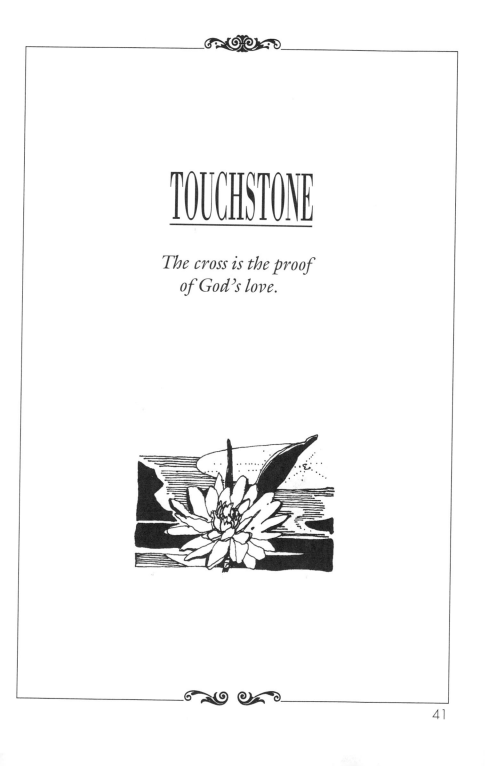

But love your enemies, do good to them.

Luke 6:35

Defusing Hostility

It is a hard moment to forget. I had just become senior pastor at First Baptist Church of Atlanta after a time of controversy. As I stood in the pulpit at a meeting, one of the men approached me and struck me. That was only one of many incidents where the displeasure and anger of others were displayed.

Did I have a hard time dealing with my emotions? You bet. Did Jesus' command to love my enemies seem an impossible command? Certainly. But I discovered, and so can you, that the love of Christ can override our emotions and prime our will to obey.

David's awkward relationship with King Saul helped me learn how to treat those who hurt or mistreat me. Thoroughly misunderstood and relentlessly pursued, David spent years in crags and caves while Saul enjoyed all the perks of kingship. Twice, David had golden opportunities to slay his tormentor. David, however, refused to exercise that option of hate, choosing instead to demonstrate his innocence and loyalty.

David did not retaliate. If we are wise, we will travel the same route. Anytime we seek revenge, subtly or blatantly, we foil the power of God's love. Retaliation takes the matter out of God's providential hand and puts it in our sinful grasp. It violates God's law of love, which Peter defines this way: "Do not repay evil with evil or insult with insult, but with blessing" (1 Peter 3:9).

How do you not return the blow you've received? By taking refuge in the sovereignty of God. Jesus, when hanging on a cross, "did not retaliate; when he suffered, he made no threats. Instead, he entrusted himself to him who judges justly" (1 Peter 2:23). Both David and the Messiah made God their hiding place from the schemes of wicked men, trusting him to handle their hurts.

Better yet, entrusting yourself and your particular circumstance to God frees you to extend grace to the offending party. Love flowed from the cross. David spoke graciously and courteously to Saul, keeping hate at bay. Do good to those who wrong you. Speak kindly to them, and the gripping thoughts of retaliation will eventually slacken.

The noblest expression of love is to give it to those who don't deserve it. That is what Jesus did when he gave himself up for us, and aren't we called to be like him? Love your enemy, and your faith will never seem more real. You can do it because God is in control.

Lord, I readily admit my difficulty in holding my temper at bay whenever I am wronged by others. The need to "get even" can become so overwhelming, I sometimes feel out of control. Fill my thoughts with your words of love spoken to others. Whenever I see others who have offended me, prompt my spirit to speak kindly to them. I can do this only through the strength of your Holy Spirit.

TOUCHSTONE

Before expressing anger, ask yourself, "What would Jesus do?"

Man looks at the outward appearance, but the LORD looks at the heart.

1 Samuel 16:7

The Big Picture

Great Bible characters weren't always so great. Moses and Peter had very inauspicious beginnings. David encountered serious obstacles, some of his own making, throughout his life. Gideon started slowly, fared well for a season, and ended with some question marks.

That's significant to me and to you because it reveals some crucial facts about the Christian life that affect our ability to personally embrace God's love.

It tells us that God is as interested in the process as he is in the result. Those who trust in Christ as Savior will arrive safely in heaven. Jesus' performance on the cross settles that issue. This means that the process of becoming like Christ is what God is primarily up to in our short span on earth. This involves failure and success, joy and grief, wisdom and foolishness, peace and turmoil. Certainly, if you were to chart the lives of Moses and David, the graph would resemble a mountain-range silhouette. God wants you to exhibit and express the life of Christ, and that is a lifelong process.

It also tells us that God is concerned with progress, not perfectionism. The men and women that God used in Scripture and the people he uses today are far from faultless. What God does care about is a heart that is bent toward obedience to him, repentant when wrong, contrite when disobedient, humbled when overreliant on self. Progress includes failure, but it moves toward a growing relationship with the Savior. God put up with David's antics because the rudder of David's heart was set toward him. Probably what impresses and encourages me the most when I think about these men is this—God saw their huge potential for godliness and waited patiently for it to develop. What farmer discards a half-grown crop? He waters, watches, and protects it until harvest. When God saves you, he knows your tremendous spiritual potential. Peter's initial vacillations paled in comparison to his later loyalty and commitment. Moses' forty years of exile were but preparation for forty years of tough leadership.

If you know God is interested in the process, looks for ultimate progress, and sees unlimited potential, you can be liberated to walk and act under the umbrella of his love. God's commitment is for eternity, but he is with you today to help you make the most of each opportunity. If you falter or fail, he will correct you and help you walk upright again. When you look at life from this perspective, it encourages you to continue the journey and keeps your blunders under the overview of unconditional love and unending grace.

Gracious Father, I am so grateful that you see my life as one big picture with one magnificent plan. As much as I don't like valley experiences, it helps to know that you have not given up on me. I don't have to feel good only on the mountain tops. You are so good. I just want to thank you, Lord, for having the big picture in mind.

TOUCHSTONE

*Today— it doesn't have to be
 perfect. Just keep the big
 picture in mind.*

Though your sins are like scarlet, they shall be as white as snow; though they are red as crimson, they shall be like wool.

Isaiah 1:18

Red and White

While working in my photographic dark room one day, I made an interesting discovery, casting the prophet Isaiah's description of sin in a revealing light. I occasionally use colored filters over my lenses when I photograph in black and white. For instance, a light yellow filter darkens the sky, while brightening the clouds. A red filter enhances the white still more. That particular day, I experimented with viewing a red dot on white paper through a red filter. To my amazement, the dot, when seen through the red filter, appeared white.

At that moment I realized the overwhelming truth of God's forgiveness. Our sin, depicted as deep red by Isaiah, becomes white as snow and wool when seen through the red cross of Golgotha. This is the great transformation of forgiveness. Jesus, the Lamb of God, took away our iniquity when his blood was shed on the cross. Our past sins, today's transgressions, and tomorrow's disobedience have been fully forgiven by Christ's once-and-for-all sacrifice. By his own doing, God in Christ has cleansed you from every stain of sin. Though you still suffer damaging consequences when you sin, you are never treated as a sinner by the Father. You are a new creation in Christ, a saint, a holy one born of God.

God's forgiveness not only takes your sins away but also credits the righteousness of Christ to your account. This is a dynamic aspect of forgiveness that is often overlooked. No blame can ever be laid to your account, because you have been justified, declared "not guilty" by the Judge himself.

God is free to express the wonder of his love to you. There is no barrier, no hindrance, for the justice of God has been satisfied. Forgiveness pulls the plug on guilt. If you are fully and freely forgiven, why put yourself on an unnecessary guilt trip? The Holy Spirit will indeed convict you of sin, but you will never stand guilty before God.

This is how God sees you—pure as snow, white as wool. Your sins have been permanently cleansed through the shed blood of Christ. Since this is how he views you, shouldn't you see yourself in the same light?

> *Father, I get overwhelmed whenever I discover your truths being reinforced through simple objects and events. I can witness miracles and your promises being fulfilled by simply opening my eyes to your creation every day. Knowing that you see me as pure, whole, and blameless seems a miracle in itself. I want to thank you and praise you for your perfect, living example of love.*

TOUCHSTONE

See yourself as God does.

My times are in your hands.

Psalm 31:15

Let It Go

Do you sometimes wrestle with God over an issue you desperately want solved? The need is urgent, the time is short, your prayers are intense. However, God seems tight-lipped. At times, there appears to be an almost inverse relationship between the magnitude of the problem and the clarity of the response from God. The more we want to know God's mind, the less he appears to reveal a solution.

After several such episodes in my life, I came to understand a potent scriptural truth that can unleash the full weight of God's power on one's behalf. Its dynamic meaning became clear only after I had come to the end of my resources. It is the principle of relinquishment.

When I reach my wit's end, when I have prayed as precisely as I know how, followed all the commands I know to obey, sought as much counsel as I thought necessary, and still have no clear guidance, I realize I must relinquish the entire situation to the Father. Never have I experienced such peace and such profoundly supernatural answers as when I relinquish the problem to God.

By relinquishment, I do not mean resignation or passivity. I am not suggesting a mind-set that centers on inaction. What I do mean is the cessation of a demanding spirit, the quieting of inner strife, the cancellation of my own agenda, and a complete willingness to settle for God's provision.

Christ himself is our example as he passionately communed with the Father regarding his death. "My Father, if it is possible, may this cup be taken from me. Yet not as I will, but as you will" (Matt. 26:39). Jesus knew his mission of redemption was incomplete without the cross, yet he still had to surrender his desires to the Father. It was a prayer of relinquishment, arrived at only after ardent, earnest petition. But what power flowed from the answer

—the cross of Christ, the crux of Christianity. Jesus, as always, said yes to the Father, and the shackles of sin were shattered.

The same principle releases God's amazing answers today. We submit to the Father's plan, whatever that may be. We give the matter over to the love of God and trust him for results that we may or may not like. Whatever the answer, it is from God; and that is all we need to know.

Relinquishing a troublesome matter to God means we have placed the dilemma squarely into the hands of God, whose goodness, wisdom, and power never fail. They are good hands.

Dear heavenly Father, I do have worrisome matters that plague me. I have tried to manipulate my circumstances, control others, and bargain with you. It has all been frivolous. Right now I want to give my circumstances to you. With open hands, I lay them before you, not holding on to any part of them. By faith, I am trusting you completely with my needs.

TOUCHSTONE

You can let go of your problem because God doesn't let go of you.

Being confident of this, that he who began a good work in you will carry it on to completion until the day of Christ Jesus.

Philippians 1:6

No Complaints

Some of my fondest memories of childhood are of my mother. My father died when I was nine months old, so my mom supported the two of us for many years. She worked the swing shift at a textile mill, coming home late each night. We didn't have very many worldly possessions. In fact, we moved frequently, living in seventeen houses over a period of sixteen years.

Yet my mother seldom complained. She always expressed confidence in God to meet our needs, and she spread cheer wherever she went. Her enthusiasm and faith were contagious.

I can't help but think of her every time I read an engaging verse of Scripture tucked away in the second chapter of Philippians: "Do everything without complaining or arguing" (Phil. 2:14).

In seven concise, potent words, Paul unveils the lifestyle that repels bitterness, regret, and anger and promotes love. To be honest, I sometimes wonder how we can obey that command when confronted with situations that seem primed to bring out the worst in us.

Yet when I think of my mother and the many difficult situations she faced without a hint of murmuring, I believe I now understand her secret to a contented, thankful heart. It is not a secret really, for it is a principle that every believer can practice successfully.

It is found in the verse immediately preceding Paul's command to tackle life with a hearty spirit: "For it is God who works in you to will and to act according to his good purpose" (Phil. 2:13).

We must never lose sight of the tremendous truth that God is constantly and positively at work in each detail of our lives. He is never limited by circumstances, never perplexed over problems. He is actively moving in our inner being to conform us to Christ's image and is sovereignly steering events toward our good and his praise.

We can genuinely give thanks in everything (1 Thess. 5:16), because God is at work in all things. Why grumble or complain if God is in control and accomplishing his purposes? I am convinced that it was because my mother understood this principle that she was enabled to go about her duties with a grateful heart.

Do you see God at work in you? If so, then each assignment of the day, great or small, bears his imprint. Refuse to yield to a critical or complaining spirit because to do so is to actually grumble against God himself (Ex. 16:8).

A thankful spirit promotes peace and health. It acknowledges God's love and affirms your trust in him. And it is a solid testimony to others that the God you serve is able, caring, and very wise.

> *God, forgive me for grumbling and com-plaining about so many things. There is much to be thankful for. I know a grateful heart promotes peace, and that is what I want. I give you permission to change my critical spirit and replace it with thanksgiving.*

TOUCHSTONE

Complaining is to the devil
what praise is to God.

Come to me, all you who are weary and burdened, and I will give you rest.

Matthew 11:28

Cease Striving

It was 2:20 A.M. I suddenly awakened from a restful sleep, sensing God had something to say to me. In a matter of seconds, Psalm 46 came to mind. I turned on the light and began to read. Although I am very familiar with this magnificent, comforting psalm, I read it deliberately and prayerfully.

The tenth verse arrested my soul: "Be still and know that I am God." In the quiet of the night, I knew God was revealing something that I desperately needed to know. I prayed, asking God to open up the meaning of the verse so that I might receive his fullness, and then I returned to bed.

The next morning I met with a group of pastors. As we prayed together, I shared my experience with one. He opened his Bible and read Psalm 46:10 from another translation (NASB): "Cease striving and know that I am God."

As soon as I heard the words "cease striving," I knew what God was saying to me. Though I know better, I have a tendency to strive in my own strength and energy. Let me tell you, that's exhausting, frustrating, and ultimately not very productive in God's scheme. As long as you think you have to perform a certain way to please God, you are in subtle conflict with him.

I breathed a sigh of spiritual relief as I saw the futility of my attempts to carry out God's commands with my resources and his amazing adequacy for every demand. I can "cease striving" to be holy and righteous, because "in Christ" I already am holy and righteous. I don't have to strain to gain God's approval, because he already loves me unconditionally.

Do you see how this removes the struggle? Do you understand how this can help you to relax and rest in the all-sufficiency of God's grace? Christ, who indwells you through the Holy Spirit, is your peace, strength, comfort, wisdom, hope, joy, and guide. You have all this because you have Christ.

You work diligently "with all his energy which so powerfully works in [you]" (Col. 1:29). You plan wisely, but with the knowledge that God's will is preeminent (Prov. 16:9). You pray fervently, but with the knowledge that God's response is always best (Jer. 33:3).

We "cease striving" when we "know that [he is] God." We don't have to white-knuckle it through life, because our sovereign God is in control. We don't have to bend beneath life's emotional load, because our loving God invites us to cast our cares on him. We don't have to manipulate our circumstances, because our wise God has a good and kind plan. We don't have to yield to our weaknesses, because our omnipotent God strengthens us for every trial and temptation.

> *God, I relinquish _____ to you. I have tried to solve the problem my way and find myself exhausted. I will accept your solution and cease striving for my own. You know this matter has greatly troubled me. It is not easy to give it over to you. But I choose to let it go and cast my burden on you.*

TOUCHSTONE

*God has provided everything
I need through Christ
and his work on the cross.*

Yet I hold this against you: You have forsaken your first love.
Revelation 2:4

The Priority
of Relationship

Are you as much in love with Jesus as you were when you first met him? That is the kind of question that can take your breath away, isn't it? It cuts to the core of the Christian life. Is your relationship with Jesus your priority, or have you become immersed in superficial service that has all the trappings of Christianity without the thrill and vitality of personal fellowship?

If you have a nagging sense that your fellowship with Christ has slowly cooled and dropped to lukewarm, then you need to consider these questions: Is Jesus still "your first love"? Does God still excite you? Is time spent in Scripture rewarding? Is telling others about the Savior fascinating? Do you begrudge giving God a tithe of your income? Your responses reveal much about the quality of your relationship with Jesus. Knowing him as your first love means you are increasingly excited about his character, his ways, and his Word.

Activity, though essential to practical faith, is not a substitute for personal fellowship. It can never outweigh intimacy with God. Our relationship with Christ erodes and cools when our primary focus is taken off the Messiah and placed on other things. That is the beginning of idolatry, and it is a dangerous path for the saint to tread. The gods of this age—sports, work, money—are cleverly disguised and ensnare many Christians with their compelling allegiance. Too much of a good thing can be wrong if it distracts you from devotion to Christ.

How can you recapture that first love? Remember what Christ did for you when you were saved, the supernatural transformation that took you from death to life, from darkness to light, from the dominion of sin to the reign of Christ. Repent of whatever has dampened your love for Jesus. Turn away from all that distracts you. Spend time in prayer and study with the single purpose of encountering God—listening, worshiping, obeying.

As a young Christian I was introduced to the writings of Oswald Chambers, who put one's relationship with Christ above all else. In his book *The Moral Foundations of Life*, Chambers wrote, "Never allow anything to fuss your relationship to Jesus Christ, neither Christian work, nor Christian blessing, nor Christian anything. Jesus Christ first, second, and third, and God himself by the great indwelling power of the Spirit within will meet the strenuous effort on your part and slowly and surely you will form the mind of Christ and become one with him as he was one with the Father."

How easy it is, Lord, to drift in my relationship with you. I'm not sure how I got to this point of mediocrity, but I want to return to you, my first love. Take away whatever has diluted my fellowship with you. May you truly be "first, second, and third" in my life. Refocus the gaze of my soul that I may see you at work in all things.

TOUCHSTONE

*First love gives God
first place.*

[Paul] traveled through that area, speaking many words of encouragement to the people.

Acts 20:2

An Encouraging Word

The words are still hung and framed neatly and permanently. Not on my wall, but in my mind. They were spoken when I was only six years old. One memorable day, as I was leaving my school room, I overheard my teacher comment to another, "I like Charles." It was the first time a person other than my mom had ever said she liked me. I was elated. Her three simple words were high-octane emotional fuel that boosted my confidence and even changed the way I viewed myself.

Have you ever thought how influential the words you speak are? Do you know what kind of impact your speech can have on a person who desperately needs to hear an encouraging word? Solomon wrote, "Pleasant words are a honeycomb, sweet to the soul and healing to the bones" (Prov. 16:24). What a wonderful way to describe our conversation. It can be medicine to a weary soul, healing to a bruised spirit. Kind words, spoken in due season, are God's bridges of love.

If you've been on the receiving end of gracious comments, you know the power of well-chosen words. Perhaps a coach noticed you at practice one day and remarked how well you had performed. Or maybe a co-worker came to you and commended your work and attitude on a difficult task. Paul describes such speech as "full of grace, seasoned with salt" (Col. 4:6). Our remarks, he says, are to be flavored with gentleness and loving-kindness, key ingredients of grace-filled speech.

The love of Christ can leap into the hearts of others through your words when you speak to them the way you want them to speak to you. Let words of cheer and praise be the order of the day, and you'll be amazed how you can change the atmosphere of your home or office. The golden rule is never more effective than when it regulates our speech.

Ask God to make you aware of the needs of others. When we are completely absorbed in our problems or activities, complimentary words rarely grace our conversation. Accept others the way they are and allow God to change them through his Spirit. Your focus is on edification, not condemnation. Your speech is targeted for "building others up according to their needs, that it may benefit those who listen" (Eph. 4:29).

Let your tongue be God's instrument of love. Speak words that young girls and boys and men and women in your neighborhood, your office, your home, your church, your school can't wait to hear.

Heavenly Father, speak through me words of encouragement and cheer. Make me sensitive to the needs of others around me, while taking my eyes off of self.

TOUCHSTONE

*Speak to others the way you
want someone to speak
to you!*

May the Lord direct your hearts into God's love.
                                    2 Thessalonians 3:5

Lovers of God

Jesus had many harsh words for the religious Jews of his day. Members of groups like the Pharisees and Sadducees relied on peer-pleasing appearances and culturally accepted norms of behavior for their approval. They were like many individuals today who conform to external standards of religion but lack any vital union with the person of Christ.

Jesus Christ described such men with one sweeping but profound statement when he addressed a proud, belligerent crowd in Jerusalem: "I know you. I know that you do not have the love of God in your hearts" (John 5:42). Their formality, their desire to please men rather than God was but a visible symptom of a basic spiritual deficiency—they did not love God nor hold him in awe in their hearts.

How would you describe yourself as a Christian? Are you a follower of Christ? Are you someone who obeys the Scripture? While these certainly are solid working definitions of a believer, would you call yourself a lover of God? When you love God rightly and sincerely, it is amazing how everything else in the Christian life fits.

The Jews had a myriad of laws and regulations that governed their distant, cold knowledge of God. Jesus shattered that legalistic maze when he said that the two greatest commandments are that we love God with all our heart and our neighbor as ourselves (Mark 12:30–31). The accumulation of thousands of years of lifeless laws was, in a matter of seconds, reduced to the essence of Christianity. Jesus knew that when a person loves God, he doesn't waste his time worshiping insignificant and trivial pursuits. He understood that a person who loves his neighbor won't murder, steal, engage in adultery, or fabricate lies. Loving God and others fulfills the law.

If you are a lover of God, you seek intimate fellowship with him. You covet his approval, while accepting the acknowledgment of others with humility. A lover of God seeks to know him, accepting his blessings simply as gracious gifts. A lover of God reads and studies the Scripture to encounter Christ personally.

Saint Augustine penned this intriguing thought: "Love God and do as you please." That sounds irresponsible at first glance, doesn't it? However, think about it, and you will agree that the person who truly loves God will act out of a heart that delights in pleasing the Father.

Are you a lover of God? If so, then you are a man or woman after God's own heart.

Lord, I do love you. I may not know exactly how to express my love, but I know I can count on you to instruct me through your Word. I ask you, Lord, that you will supernaturally empower me to love others as Christ loves them. Guard my intentions, that they will not be misunderstood. Let others see Jesus, not me.

TOUCHSTONE

*Love God, and you will do
what pleases him.*

Let us ... love with actions and in truth.

1 John 3:18

Love in Action

He was my Sunday school teacher, and a good one. But I remember him for something else. Craig Stowe would stop me on the street while I was on my paper route and purchase a newspaper. He would spend five or ten minutes chatting, asking me about my family, school, and things that matter to a young boy. Not only that, he always gave me more than what the newspaper cost. It didn't take me long to figure out that Craig Stowe didn't need to buy a newspaper . . . he got the newspaper at home.

What that man did each week for several years demonstrated God's love to me. He went out of his way to show that he wasn't just my Sunday school teacher. He involved himself in my life in a tangible fashion, and I will never forget him.

Kind words are gentle healers, but kind deeds are megadoses of the love of Christ. Jesus didn't just say he loved us; he demonstrated his love by dying for us (Rom. 5:8). Only hours before he was to die, Jesus told his disciples that the world would know they were his followers by their love for each other (John 13:35). He obviously meant they would have a lifestyle that visibly and practically expressed God's love.

Barnabas became involved with a discouraged young man named Mark, who later penned one of the gospels. Mary and Martha showed their love for Christ by inviting him to dine and rest in their home in Bethany. Paul reminded Titus that Christ's death not only saved us from sin but should be the motivation for us to be "eager to do what is good" (Titus 2:14). We are even "created in Christ Jesus to do good works" (Eph. 2:10).

So go ahead and bake that pie for the mom who just arrived home from the hospital. Mow that yard for the elderly man whose arthritis has almost immobilized him. Invite that lonely person from the Sunday school class out to lunch. Take time for a coffee break with that frustrated co-worker. Help the new neighbor unload the boxes that are still in his garage. Write that encouraging note to the young man or woman who is struggling to adapt to the college routine.

Sharing God's love in this manner incarnates the compassion of Christ and says "I care" louder than any words possibly could. All it takes is a willing spirit to lift another believer. Nothing but good comes from doing good.

Lord, I've been a little slothful with my idle time lately. I worry about my own problems so much that I forget that others around me have needs as well. Show me how to demonstrate your concern to others around me. Thank you for the memories of times when others have gone out of their way to show me special attention. These memories have always been a boost when I've been down.

TOUCHSTONE

Actions say more than you think.

I will . . . praise your name for your love and your faithfulness.
Psalm 138:2

When We Praise

The more you love God, the more you will worship him. Love and praise are natural partners. Heaven is a place where those who love God live in constant praise of him. Should your present experience be any different?

We praise God for what he has done. "Praise him for his acts of power," writes the enthusiastic psalmist in Psalm 150:2. His "acts of power" are the extraordinary events recorded in Scripture—creation, miracles, the cross, the resurrection. They also are the remarkable displays of his personal love for you. Why not write down some of the ways that God has demonstrated his power in your life? Think of his guidance, his provision, his protection, and the numerous other ways he has supplied your personal needs. A journal that records God's handiwork in your life is a tremendous launching pad for joyful praise.

We praise God for "his surpassing greatness" (Ps. 150:2). This is pure praise, standing in awe of God for who he is. He is faithful. He is kind. He is good. He is just. He is holy. He is patient. He is generous. God acts greatly because he is a great God. His character and attributes should overwhelm us. Our response should be nothing short of ecstatic gratitude. Think of this: you have the opportunity to praise a personal, perfect God who takes great interest in who you are and what you do.

Praise magnifies God and puts problems into perspective. What obstacle is too big for God? What circumstance is too perplexing for him? Many times I have come to God with a consuming burden, only to find it light and easy after a session of praise and worship.

Praise reveals our devotion to Christ. Habakkuk the prophet wrote that he would praise God even in the worst of times, when the "olive crop fails and the fields produce no food, though there are no sheep in the pen and no cattle in the stalls" (Hab. 3:17).

Even if you are caught in such a worst-case scenario, God still deserves your praise. And from experience, I can tell you that praise is the one factor that will deliver you from the sinkhole of depression and discouragement.

Express your love for Christ by putting a priority on praise. Make it a point to enter his presence with a thankful heart before you present your requests. Choose to praise in difficult straits. It makes all the difference, because it focuses on the God who makes the difference.

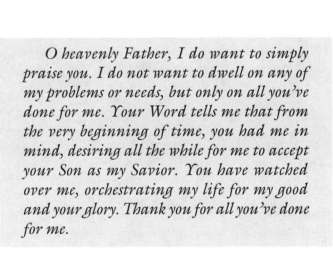

O heavenly Father, I do want to simply praise you. I do not want to dwell on any of my problems or needs, but only on all you've done for me. Your Word tells me that from the very beginning of time, you had me in mind, desiring all the while for me to accept your Son as my Savior. You have watched over me, orchestrating my life for my good and your glory. Thank you for all you've done for me.

TOUCHSTONE

Praise fuels love's engine.

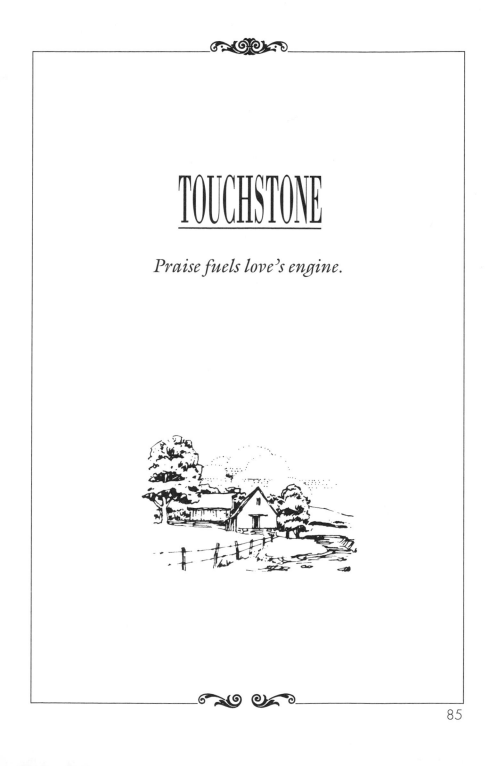

No one can snatch them out of my hand.

John 10:28

That Loving Feeling

Sir Winston Churchill once remarked that it was dangerous to "always [be] feeling one's pulse and taking one's temperature." His words were addressed to those who looked at the wildly fluctuating fortunes of battle to determine England's success or failure in World War II.

His words are apropos as well for the Christian who constantly gauges his relationship with Christ based on feelings. Emotions are unreliable barometers, and if you attach your faith to them, you are in for an upsetting experience. Certainly, we are to love God and do those things that please him, such as reading his Word, spending time in prayer, and joining with a local body of believers. But there are occasions when the Bible seems cold, our prayers listless, our commitment to the church uncertain; and if we allow our feelings to govern our fellowship with Christ in these instances, we are sure to drift into self-condemning, guilt-ridden waters.

The crux of the matter is not relying on your degree of love for God for stability and security. This is much like holding the proverbial wrong end of the stick. The prescription to a steady, progressive walk of faith is focusing on God's love for you. His love is unchanging and fixed forever.

Think about this illustration: Imagine your hand and God's clasped together. Your grip loosens during a season of temptation, sin, doubt, or apathy. Your feelings of love for God are minimal. But rather than concentrating on your slackness, look to the hand of God. His grip of love is solid. He will not let go. "Your right hand upholds me," declared David in the forlorn deserts of Judah (Ps. 63:8). "For I am the LORD, your God, who takes hold of your right hand," said God to a fearful people (Isa. 41:13).

You are eternally secure in the love of God. You are sealed by the Holy Spirit with the unperturbed life of Christ. Heaven is reserved for you. In this light, you can cease, as Churchill said, from the paralysis of morbid introspection. You can stop depending on your irregular spiritual pulse as an indicator of your love relationship with Christ.

The favorable winds of God's love for you blow continuously. Move forward in that truth, and the turbulence of gusty emotions will not blow you off your course of growing in the grace and knowledge of Jesus Christ.

I can be so easily influenced by my feelings, and the results of my actions can be so devastating, Lord. Strengthen my faith walk with you. My heart's desire is to grasp your hand firmly at all times. Teach me to overcome feelings that are damaging to our relationship. Thank you, Father, for your steadfast love.

TOUCHSTONE

Nothing can loosen God's grip on you.

For God loves a cheerful giver.

2 Corinthians 9:7

To Give

When I consider a scriptural synonym for *love*, I am drawn to the constant biblical use of the word *give*. "For God so loved the world that he *gave* his one and only Son . . ." (John 3:16). "I live by faith in the Son of God, who loved me and *gave* himself for me" (Gal. 2:20).

God gives you the gift of salvation and the Holy Spirit. He gives peace, strength, and wisdom to those who ask.

It is impossible to love someone without giving. We bestow our affection on family members and friends with various forms of giving. We demonstrate our commitment to Christ and others by giving our time, our resources, our energies. Generosity is the hallmark of genuine Christianity. "A generous man will prosper; he who refreshes others will himself be refreshed" (Prov. 11:25). Giving is the channel through which the love of God flows.

"But I have so little to give," you lament. That may be true, but as long as you wait until you have a surplus to give, you will never begin. A generous person primes the pump by giving even the little things—a listening ear, a tip for the grocery boy, a handmade gift for Christmas.

A generous person is happy. Others are drawn to a generous person, not for a handout, but because of the inviting spiritual atmosphere that surrounds him. A generous person is sensitive to the needs of others and gives genuinely, not for the purpose of manipulation. He receives joy in seeing others benefit from his benevolence. He views needs as an opportunity, not a threat. He wants to see how much he can give, not how little. He trusts God for his own needs.

Why is giving so important? Because it is the sure cure for greed, the antithesis of generosity. God blesses generosity and curses greed. Giving is the antidote for selfishness, a lifestyle that cannot reflect the likeness of the indwelling Christ.

Generosity opens the heart of both giver and recipient to the lavish love of Christ. Both can become spiritually wealthy and prosperous, enjoying the riches of the Christ-centered life. If you are reluctant to give, stingy with your resources, and isolated from the needs of others, you're missing out on fantastic blessings from your generous heavenly Father. "Give and it will be given to you," Jesus promised (Luke 6:38). Such is the power of generosity. It is the right choice to make. Give something today and watch God work.

Jesus, the first step is the hardest to take. Giving any amount or any thing appears sacrificial at this point. But I've read these words and I've listened to the testimonies of others that reveal the blessings that come from heartfelt giving. Today, show me a way in which I may give of myself to benefit others and glorify you.

TOUCHSTONE

It's impossible to love
without giving.

For Christ's love compels us.

2 Corinthians 5:14

Fish and Sheep

Peter had fished all night and came away empty-handed. It was now early morning, and the rhythmic lapping of waves against his boat made Peter all the more drowsy. Yet the intriguing words of Jesus as he taught from Peter's boat kept him awake.

"When [Jesus] had finished speaking, he said to Simon, 'Put out into deep water, and let down the nets for a catch'" (Luke 5:4). There is reluctance and weariness in Peter's response: "Master, we've worked hard all night, but because you say so, I will let down the nets." We know the rest of the story. The catch of Peter's life nearly took the boat down, and Peter learned an unforgettable lesson in obedience.

However, there was more to discover. Later Jesus, in his resurrected body, is again on the shore by the sea. Peter, sharing a meal with his risen Lord, is confronted by Christ: "Simon son of John, do you truly love me more than these?" (John 21:15). The question befuddles Peter. "Of course, you know that I love you Jesus," he replies. Twice more, Jesus queries Peter about his love for the Messiah. Peter reaffirms his commitment each time and finally receives this command from the Savior: "Feed my sheep" (v. 17).

This dramatic postresurrection dialogue with the Lord underscored a new beginning for Peter. The rough-hewn fisherman would no longer obey just because Jesus told him what to do, as in the Sea of Galilee encounter (Luke 5:5). He would not adhere to Jesus' words only because he was the Master, the Savior, the Lord.

Something greater was at stake. Peter's obedience, his future evangelization of other lands, and his leadership in the Judean church were to be motivated by love for Christ. Our obedience validates our love, but our discipleship is always prompted by devoted love for the Savior. Obedience that issues forth from love is a delight, not a burden; and it is the pure wellspring of the abundant life.

Do you obey God from duty or fear, or do you follow and serve Christ out of a heart filled with love? When the love of Christ "compels you," you are on the right road to godliness. Your relationship to Christ is the priority, and obedience is merely the follow-through.

Peter needed to reexamine his motivation for obedience. Jesus asked tough questions to prepare Peter for tough times. He will sift you as well if you allow him to, so that your obedience will spring from love.

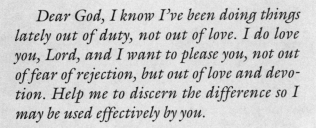

Dear God, I know I've been doing things lately out of duty, not out of love. I do love you, Lord, and I want to please you, not out of fear of rejection, but out of love and devotion. Help me to discern the difference so I may be used effectively by you.

TOUCHSTONE

The springs of obedience have
their fountainhead
in love.

For great is your love toward me.

Psalm 86:13

Just for You

Our culture continues to grow increasingly impersonal. Perhaps, like me, you've been shopping in a large store and found it almost impossible to locate someone to assist you. The notion of personalized service in any sector is virtually archaic. And have you noticed how people are treated in generalities, classified by income level or categorized into a particular age group?

This kind of depersonalization bothers me. That's why it thrills me to know that God loves me as an individual. He does not think of me or you in generic terms, but has specific thoughts toward us as unique persons.

Jesus came to Bethany to resurrect Lazarus. Mary and Martha had earlier sent word to the Messiah about their brother: "Lord, the one you love is sick" (John 11:3). Lazarus was not just another person among the multitudes to Christ. He was a man whom Christ loved as a friend. Later, as Jesus approached Lazarus's tomb, he was moved to tears. "See how he loved him!" marveled those assembled nearby (v. 36).

Jesus loves you just as personally. He is interested in you, your hobbies, your vocation, your emotions, your needs. He knows you as distinct from all others. "You know when I sit and when I rise; you perceive my thoughts from afar. . . . You are familiar with all my ways" (Ps. 139:2–3). God's intimate acquaintance with David, all of his ways and quirks, moved David to amazement. We should be no less staggered.

Biblical expressions like "the apple of your eye" and "engraved on the palm of your hand" are God's ways of describing his incredibly personal affection for you (Ps. 17:8; Isa. 49:16).

Such love means that the Father has a plan for you that no one else can fulfill. Although his ultimate goal of conforming you to Christ's image remains constant, he has custom-designed events, circumstances, and relationships that will lead you into his will. He works in your inner being and in the routine of your life in a divinely original manner. He knows exactly what you need, when you need it. He knows your frame—how much pressure you can stand, your personality makeup, the composition of your soul.

Since God deals with you as an individual, your personal thoughts, words, and actions are of great importance, for you matter to God. You are uppermost on God's mind today. Isn't that fantastic!

It's good to know I have such an intimate Friend as you, Jesus. Because of your omnipotence, I can trust you to lead me through the dark shadows of life. I know you will always be right beside me. And because you are omniscient, you are aware of my innermost feelings better than I usually am. Thank you, dear Friend.

TOUCHSTONE

*God has a job for me that no
one else is qualified for.*

There is no fear in love. But perfect love drives out fear.

1 John 4:18

Banish Fear

Faith in God is frequently presented as the corrective for fear. There is no doubt that even a small dose of trust can move great mountains of phobias and anxiety. That is why I find the apostle John's prescription so fascinating. Love, John says, is the way to banish fear. In a strict sense, John speaks about love removing the fear of punishment, the fear of offending an angry God. But it is just as applicable to the entire emotional spectrum of fears and worries that trouble us. The Amplified Version gives the expanded meaning: "Full-grown (complete, perfect) love turns fear out of doors and expels every trace of terror."

John does not exclude faith as an ally when dealing with fear, but he stresses that love is an even greater spiritual weapon. Having faced many fears of my own, I understand his rationale. When we are afraid, faith seems distant. Fear wreaks such havoc with our emotions that trust seems unobtainable, unreachable. We want to have faith, but we appear quite faithless. Yet when we think of God's love for us in frightening times, great peace and comfort settle within. When we think of God's care for us, his absolute commitment to our entire well-being, "every trace of terror" can be exiled.

Perfect love is God's provision. Jesus said, "My grace is sufficient" (2 Cor. 12:9). The love of Christ is enough to conquer the source of any fear. Are you afraid of failure? God's love never fails. Are you afraid of the future? God's love has already provided for your tomorrows.

Perfect love is God's protection. You are held steadfast by God. He is a sure refuge and fortress to those who turn to him. God, who never slumbers, is the keeper of your soul. He is a sovereign hedge about you, allowing only those things to touch you that are first filtered through his love.

Perfect love is God's presence. God is with you in every situation. He abides in you so you can face each fear in the confident awareness that Jesus is Immanuel—God with us, and therefore God with you.

As you learn more about God's provision, protection, and presence, fear dissipates. His perfect love enfolds and encompasses you. The better you grasp his love, the easier it becomes to trust him. Kick fear "out of doors" where it belongs and replace it with the certainty that your loving God is taking perfect care of you.

The LORD is my shepherd, I shall not be in want. . . . Even though I walk through the valley of the shadow of death, I will fear no evil, for you are with me; your rod and your staff, they comfort me. . . . Surely goodness and love will follow me all the days of my life, and I will dwell in the house of the LORD forever. (Psalm 23)

TOUCHSTONE

God's love is never-ending,
his protection ever-present.

Those whom I love I rebuke and discipline.

Revelation 3:19

Tough Love

God's love is not all fuzzy and warm. If that were true, then we must conclude that it is defective. A father and mother who love their son or daughter invoke disciplinary measures when necessary. Our heavenly Father, likewise, does not hesitate to correct us with loving discipline when our behavior violates his good and gracious ways.

David met the stern love of God on several occasions for his waywardness. The psalmist learned that God wasn't all sweetness. Peter felt the sting of God's tough love as he denied Christ. Paul had harsh words for Mark after the young disciple went AWOL on his first missionary journey. Eventually, we all discover that God is serious about the business of holiness; and when hard actions are called for, he will oblige.

Perhaps you have enforced strict guidelines with a strong-willed child. Or you have had to make some tough decisions at work regarding problem employees. Whatever the circumstance, love sometimes must be expressed in stern tones to be effective.

God's discipline, however, is always motivated by love. "The Lord disciplines those he loves" (Heb. 12:6). Don't fall into a pity party when God orchestrates his correction. It is actually a reminder that he cares for you enough to keep you from self-destructing. The unbeliever is still under God's condemnation, but the Christian is never condemned, only disciplined. That is good news.

The context of God's redress is a Father/child relationship. "Endure hardship as discipline; God is treating you as sons" (Heb. 12:7). You are not a stranger, an alien to God. You are his child and, as such, you experience his fatherly correction. Do not mistake his discipline as anger and feel that your relationship with him has cruelly changed. That is Satan's lie. You have been adopted into his family, and his discipline only enables you to fully enjoy the benefits of his fatherhood.

Never forget that "God disciplines us for our good, that we may share in his holiness" (Heb. 12:10). The pain of chastisement has a purpose—to help us live more like God himself. The dross of impure motives and dubious behavior is purged by God's tough love. It is cleansing, refining, and restoring.

Do not turn away or become bitter when God's sternness is directed toward you. It is a sign of his love, and the goal is to remove unnecessary baggage and to strengthen you for the journey.

My loving Father, I know I have done things in my life that have made me seem unlovely. I can recall paying the consequences for those actions, too. I realize now that you were in it all the while, and your loving hand of discipline kept me safe from myself and matured me in my walk with you. As much as I don't like to be disciplined, I am very grateful that you love me enough to intervene in my life in such a way. Amen.

TOUCHSTONE

*God's tough love comes from
a tender heart.*

He has given us his very great and precious promises.

2 Peter 1:4

Standing on a Promise

At a crucial time in my life, when the church I pastored faced an overwhelming obstacle, God riveted my faith on this verse of Scripture: "You are the God who performs miracles; you display your power among the peoples" (Ps. 77:14). I meditated on that verse daily, applying it to the problem at hand. I wasn't sure of the outcome, but I was sure of the promise. Amazingly, God intervened and blessed the congregation with a supernatural answer.

You too can rely on the promises of God's Word. The Bible is a book of promises as well as principles. It is freighted with sparkling verses that declare God's intention to graciously bestow good gifts. Some promises are conditional; God will act in a certain way if you obey certain criteria, as in "Give, and it will be given to you" (Luke 6:38). But there are thousands of Scriptures that wait only for a ready faith and a willing spirit to claim them.

Bible promises are assertions of God's love for you. God has assumed full responsibility for meeting your needs and provides nourishing promises as one means of his supply. Claim a promise from God that applies to your particular need. If anxiety has become a part of your lifestyle, Philippians 4:6–7 and Psalm 46:10 are God's answers. You can be certain that God will fulfill his promise when the context of Scripture is not violated, when the answer to the promise glorifies God and demonstrates his character, and when the Holy Spirit quietly impresses on your heart that he is speaking to you through the specific promise.

As God's promise percolates in your heart, be patient. God operates according to his time schedule, not yours. He sees the end from the beginning and knows precisely when to act. Don't lose heart or be discouraged in the process. It may take days, months, even years for the promise to ripen, but God will keep his word. Remain focused on the promise, digesting its full meaning, letting God speak all he wants through the Scriptures. Be obedient in the daily rounds, yielded and submitted to the revealed will of God.

God's promises are anchors for your soul. They keep you grounded in his love and faithfulness, reminding you of your dependence on him. What God promises, he will fulfill. As David Livingstone, the noted missionary, said, "It is the word of a Gentleman of the most sacred and strictest honour, and there's an end on it!" Claim it as your own, and stand in faith until God replies.

Thank you, Lord, for standing behind your promises. They are reliable and trustworthy and for me. Your word is truth and I can always count on that when the need is great. Help me to learn your promises that apply to my circumstances and firmly bank on their fulfillment.

TOUCHSTONE

*God doesn't break his
promises.*

So Jacob served seven years to get Rachel, but they seemed like only a few days to him because of his love for her.

Genesis 29:20

Time Flies

It can take an entire day for me to capture the image I want for a photograph. Waiting for the right amount of light, framing the shot exactly, and taking advantage of other nuances demand time. But those outings seldom seem long or tedious to me because I love photography. Time flies when you are having fun—when you love what you are doing and are excited about the results.

Do you love what you do or do you complain? Is your heart merry, having the continual feast of happiness that Proverbs describes (Prov. 15:15), or is it weighed down with anxiety or boredom? Regardless of the dullness or monotony of your surroundings, I am convinced that God can transform your attitude so you can approach your tasks and relationships with a cheerful disposition.

Jim Elliot, the missionary who was later martyred, said, "Wherever you are, be all there." You may want to be in another job, another marriage, another state, another home; but the key to enjoying life is contentment with your present lot, as difficult as that may be. The grass of another job that looks green to you now looked brown to the person who left it. Godliness accompanied by contentment is a "great gain" (1 Tim. 6:6). It's fine to dream and set goals, but focus your energy on making the most of where God has put you.

Learn to view your situation from this divine perspective: "That everyone may eat and drink, and find satisfaction in all his toil—this is the gift of God" (Eccl. 3:13). Your life is a gift from God, along with all that comes with it. Even in strenuous seasons, we can discover God's merriment. When you walk up that unchanging assembly line each day or walk into the office of that perpetually irritable boss, think of your circumstances as God's gift. They may not always be wrapped in pretty packages, but the events of your life are orchestrated by the loving hand of God for your good. The joy of the Lord really can become your strength.

A proven curative for transcending the mundane to taste of God's goodness is the knowledge that God rewards your labor. Our sins have been judged; so when we stand before our Savior and Judge, we will be rewarded for our labor (2 Cor. 5:10). Every day, every action, every moment counts for eternity, for God sees your heart and motives and will recompense you.

You can learn to love what you do, to enjoy being where you are, and to be satisfied with your relationships. When that happens—and it will if you integrate these principles into your thinking—then, as with Jacob, the years will seem like only a few days, and your joy will be full.

Abba Father, you know I have been unhappy in my current situation. I've been guilty of looking at others' lives, wanting what they have, not what I have. I want to make a change . . . right now. I need your help in changing my attitude. Instill in me a happy, cheerful outlook in all that I do, understanding that this is your will for my life.

TOUCHSTONE

*The only change you may
need to make in your life
is a change in attitude.*

God our Savior ... wants all men to be saved and to come to a knowledge of the truth.

1 Timothy 2:3–4

Evangelism Made Easy

Just talk about evangelism, and most people quiver. They know they haven't been to the latest soul-winning course, and they have difficulty communicating the gospel to their family, and even more to a stranger or a friend. The thought of visiting a home and fumbling through a verbal outline brings on the spiritual shakes.

I have some good news about sharing the Good News. It doesn't require any theological training. There's nothing to memorize, and you don't have to set aside a specific night of the week to make it work. Basically, I want to take away all the excuses and focus your attention on the simple truth that love is the greatest apologetic. More people are brought into God's kingdom through a Christian's love than through any other means. Jesus said others would know about our faith and Savior when we major on love.

People in your circles of concern—family, friends, neighbors, co-workers, social acquaintances—need Christ. God has placed you in proximity to their lives to help them know the love that God has for them. It doesn't have to be strained or forced. Their turning to Christ can happen spontaneously or progressively when you are God's vessel of love to them.

Begin by accepting them as they are. They may be rowdy, uncouth, immoral, or unethical. These are natural turnoffs to the Christian, but God wants you to love them despite their actions. You cannot expect regenerate behavior from an unregenerate person. You obviously don't have to agree with their lifestyle; but by accepting the person as someone special to God, you are demonstrating the completely supernatural quality of unconditional love. Remember the darkness you once lived in before salvation and how God's love drew you into his light.

Trust in the power of the Holy Spirit to save them. You don't have to know the right words. You don't have to have a stack of special evangelism-oriented verses. God will work through your ordinary ways to express his extraordinary love. The Holy Spirit is the only person who can regenerate an unbeliever. That is his job, not yours. Your words and deeds of kindness to the non-Christian build bridges for the Holy Spirit to work. He wants them saved more than you do.

Persevere. An unbeliever can build up some sturdy walls of reasoning to ward off the gospel. It usually takes time for God's truth to triumph. But there is no wall that God's love cannot surmount, no barrier it cannot penetrate. Extend the love of God persistently to those around you, and you will never think of evangelism as hard again.

Lord, when I think back, I remember that it was the demonstration of your love through someone else that made me yearn for you. I want to make that same impact on others I come into contact with. Keep my spirit sensitive to those around me and to their needs. Help me to be a light on their pathway.

TOUCHSTONE

The Holy Spirit just wants us to be there—he will do the rest.

Be kind and compassionate to one another, . . . just as in Christ God forgave you.

Ephesians 4:32

Righting Wrongs

It was a memorable dinner—not for the food, but for the conversation. In the dining room of our home, God was righting some wrongs between my children and me. I wanted to know if there was any unforgiveness in their hearts toward me or if while rearing them I had done something that deeply hurt them.

Andy spoke first, "Dad, do you remember the time you were in your study and I was practicing some music? I had played the same part several times, and you came into the living room and said, 'Andy, is that all you know?' As far as I was concerned, you were rejecting both me and my music. That hurt." Becky jumped in, "When I was five years old and we lived in Miami, you sent me to my room and made me stay there. I cried and cried."

Those were just the first shots fired over the bow. They shared other instances when I had offended them. Now, I could have defended myself, but I knew there was only one thing I should do—ask them to forgive me. They did, and the air of resentment and bitterness was cleared.

Whether you have wronged a person or a person has wronged you, forgiveness is the only viable option to fully experience the love of God. When you seek forgiveness or extend it, you launch Christlike love into the heart of the problem. An unforgiving spirit is poison. It stagnates Christian growth, pollutes your relationship with Jesus, and robs you of personal joy. A forgiving spirit hurdles emotional barriers and heals spiritual scars.

Start the healing process by first examining yourself and repenting of an unforgiving spirit. Thomas à Kempis wrote, "We carefully count others' offenses against us, but we rarely consider what others may suffer because of us." Continue the healing process by canceling the debt of wrongs against you. The process is emotionally charged, but it is a matter of choice, not feelings. This releases the person from your judgment just as God released you from sin's debt when he forgave you. Recognize that the offender has exposed an unforgiving bent in you that God can heal when you choose to pardon.

All time spent in the backwash of an unforgiving spirit is wasted time. It counts for nothing, advances nothing. But the moment you forgive, the restoration process begins. Bitterness loses its hostile grip, and the freedom of forgiveness is ushered in. You can never be fully free until you fully forgive.

Lord, it's incredible how past unresolved hurts can affect so much of our lives. I do not want anything to come between me and the love you have to give. I know there are hurts I must deal with and correct. Please bring to my mind those past wrongs and give me the wisdom to make them right.

TOUCHSTONE

It's never wrong to do right.

I love the LORD, for he heard my voice; he heard my cry for mercy. Because he turned his ear to me I will call on him as long as I live.

Psalm 116:1–2

Solving Problems Through Prayer

Two things are said to be certain—death and taxes. Let me add a third—problems. But unlike the first two, you can do something about the latter. You can pray. In his love, God has provided prayer as a means to forge fellowship with himself and provide access to his wisdom for our problems. God is in the problem-solving business, and when you present your dilemmas to him, he will answer. His reply may not be what you thought or wanted, and it may not fit neatly into your schedule. Nonetheless, God has entered into a covenant relationship with you whereby he assumes the awesome responsibility to help you, lead you, correct you, and make his will known to you. Prayer is the frontier of discovery.

Present your problem to God. Don't dance around what is bothering you. "God, you know the boy next door who plays the drums at midnight is annoying me and disturbing my family. Show me how to solve the problem without losing my temper." The more specific you are in prayer, the more readily you can discern his answer.

Expect God to act. God told his people to call on him and watch him do great things (Jer. 33:3). Your petitions are meaningless if you don't anticipate God's response. That is what faith is about—seeing him moving and working behind everything. Wait for the Lord's reply and remember that your problem awaits his solutions, not yours. In his essay "The Efficacy of Prayer," C. S. Lewis wrote, "If an infinitely wise Being listens to the requests of finite and foolish creatures, of course he will sometimes grant and sometimes refuse them." God's solutions are always best, even if they do not align with our desires.

Thank God during the interval. Thanksgiving acknowledges God's faithfulness and love when circumstances say otherwise. A thankful heart rejoices in the God who answers, as much as it does in the answer itself.

God is greater than your problem and is eminently able to resolve it. The power of prayer can never be overestimated because of the omnipotent God who hears and answers. Be willing to work out your difficulty his way, follow his instructions, and assume the risk that he may or may not remove the problem. In any case, your petitions will set the stage for the best possible solution, for you have put your trust in the God who cares.

> *How foolish it is of me, Father, to think I can out-think, out-plan, and out-solve an omnipotent, omniscient, omnipresent God. You know my tomorrows as well as you know my yesterdays. You know my needs before I do; and what's greatest is that you know the solutions.*

TOUCHSTONE

No problem is too big
for God.

For our light and momentary troubles are achieving for us an eternal glory that far outweighs them all.

2 Corinthians 4:17

Why, Lord?

"If God is all-powerful and all-loving, why do I suffer?"

This universal question has spanned the centuries, perplexing some, discouraging others. I do not have a prefabricated answer. The suffering I have seen and, at times, personally endured defies neatly configured definition. I can only tell you what I have discovered, what the Bible says, and trust that God will provide the necessary understanding.

It helps to realize that suffering was not part of God's original plan. There were no screams of pain, no mental impairments, no physical handicaps at creation. Neither is suffering allowed entrance into the heavenly world we one day will occupy. Suffering came with man's fall; and as long as the world and its inhabitants are in revolt against God, it must be dealt with. But our wrestling is against the backdrop of an all-powerful God who loved us enough to cast his only Son, Jesus Christ, into this caldron of trouble and woe. The Savior whom you call upon in distress is One who sympathizes with your agony and hurt, for he himself has suffered.

In this context, we recognize that suffering is inevitable but not permanent. And since our omnipotent God is truly all-loving, then even the horror and anguish of suffering must have an eventual design of good. Glance at the cross and see the blood, the jeers, the abandonment. How could God allow such a calamity? But where would we be apart from such an excruciating crucifixion? There would be no resurrection, no salvation, no hope of heaven. God, while not causing evil, does sovereignly allow it. It is never outside of his control or beyond his power to use it for good. We can actually glorify God when we respond rightly to suffering, and this itself should tell us that we can advance in our adversity.

Suffering refines our faith. The trivial is excised, the essential emphasized. Do we believe God in the face of it all? If so, we will grow and be strengthened. Suffering prepares us to comfort others. Words from smiling, indifferent faces to wounded hearts mean little; but words from a fellow sufferer support and uplift. Suffering removes artificial props of security and resets the stage of our personal world with new dependence on Christ. We cannot change the circumstance. We must trust God. As Jesus entrusted himself to the Father on the torture-rack of the cross, so we too entrust ourselves to our Savior.

Suffering is real. Don't deny it, but don't succumb to it. There is an end to it. And the God of all love can bring meaning and purpose to the darkest hour. "The God of all grace, who called you to his eternal glory in Christ, after you have suffered a little while, will himself restore you and make you strong, firm and steadfast" (1 Peter 5:10). This is God's promise to you.

There have been times in my life when I've questioned my suffering, when I've pled, "Why, Lord?" and not received a reply. Because of your sovereignty, you've allowed me an explanation for some of my sorrows, proving your protection toward me, and you have withheld explanations I may not be ready for. The hurt is real, but you can be the only comfort to me during those trying times. Though you did not author suffering, you can turn it around, giving it new meaning and purpose. And I thank you for it.

TOUCHSTONE

*Suffering is profitable when
we make the right
response.*

But the greatest of these is love.

1 Corinthians 13:13

Love Is ...

The greatest thing in the world is love. Nothing rivals its power to heal, restore, mend, and make all things new. Love surpasses all other virtues. Set into Scripture like a crown jewel, the thirteenth chapter of First Corinthians shimmers with the practical purity of love.

Love is "patient." It is never in a rush, never forceful, never demanding. It waits for God's best, whenever and whatever that may be. It refuses to yield to panic or grasp at temporal solutions.

Love is "kind." It acts in the best interest of others. It overlooks offenses. It is extravagant, giving more than what is asked or needed. Love "does not envy, it does not boast, it is not proud." It waits for God to promote and exalt. It credits him for the success and acknowledges the contributions of others. It applauds the gain of another. It does not flaunt or taunt, but bends its knee in humility.

Love is not "rude." It is polite and courteous to all, even to those who are ill-mannered or ill-tempered. Love is not "self-seeking." It does not relentlessly pursue personal perfection, but gives priority to the kingdom of God.

Love "is not easily angered and keeps no record of wrongs." It is not irritated by the behavior of others. It refuses to judge, leaving that to God. It does not keep a mental record of offenses. Love does not delight in evil, but rejoices with the truth. It meets each day with cheer and a smile. It thinks upon good things and is happy in simple obedience to God.

Love "never fails." It lasts. It works for anyone in any circumstance. It sets you free. It is always the right thing to do. When you choose to love, you have chosen God's way.

Measure your love by these attributes. When provoked or tempted, review this chapter and think on its brilliance. Let its truth light your path. If you are overwhelmed by the enormity of love, choose one of its features and commit yourself to obedience. Continually turn it over in your mind and heart until it is woven into your spirit.

If you are to reflect such love, you must put away "childish ways" (v. 11). Your goal is maturity in Christ, and the old way of living and thinking is a hindrance. God has made you a new creature, and love is the main ingredient. Renew your mind daily with the principles of God's Word, so that your emotions, intellect, and will may be greenhouses for the love of God to flourish.

Thanks for giving me such a clear description of love and its power, Father. I want these qualities to be real in my life, but I know that only you can make that happen. When I walk in love, I am wonderfully free, and that is how you want me to be.

TOUCHSTONE

*You are never more like God
than when you love.*

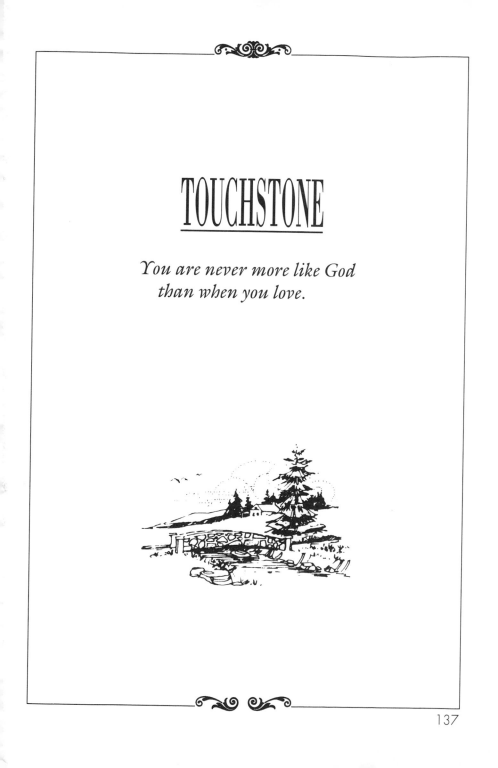